Sister Sahibs

Sister Sahibs

Marian Robertson

The Book Guild Ltd
Sussex England

*To my grandchildren, Thomas, Sarah, Edward and James
and in memory of
Verity,
my V.A.D. friend of this story,
who died on Christmas Day, 1983.*

The Book Guild Ltd
25 High Street,
Lewes, Sussex

First published 1987
© Marian Robertson 1987

Set in Linotron Cartier
Typeset by CST, Eastbourne
Printed in Great Britain by
Antony Rowe Ltd
Chippenham, Wilts

ISBN 0 86332 285 9

Acknowledgements

My grateful thanks to our Commandant Miss Corsar now Mrs Tottenham, for allowing me to use the reports that she had sent to Red Cross Headquarters in London. They now form an Appendix to this book, and give a clear, overall picture of the V.A.D.s who served under S.E. Asia Command from 1944 to 1946.

My thanks to all those who helped me, either by advice, encouragement: Especially Barry Gregory of Regimental Press, Philip Reed of the Imperial War Museum, Peter Reeve and Peter Church. Lastly my husband, without whose encouragement I might never have finished it.

The WAR IN BURMA, and the 14th ARMY

General Slim, in his book DEFEAT INTO VICTORY, gives a detailed and very readable account of the whole campaign in Burma, but here is a brief resume that will give help in the reading of this book of mine.

After the Japanese attack on Pearl Harbour and the destruction of the American fleet there, the whole of the Pacific became wide open for a lightning thrust down by the Japanese. Singapore was supposed to be impregnable by sea, but they invaded further north. They came down through Malaya and attacked from the landward side, and Singapore fell on 15 February 1942. Reinforcements of British troops had only arrived a week or so before, but they and the rest of the Garrison had to surrender, and then endure, or die, in the hell of Japanese P.O.W. camps for the next three and a half years.

Burma was quite unprepared for an invasion. The small number of R.A.F. and American Air Force at Rangoon put up an incredible fight against appalling odds, until their remainder were withdrawn to the north.

The only approach to Burma was by sea via Rangoon, as there were no railways or motor roads across the northern, natural barrier of mountains between India and Burma. When Rangoon fell on 9th March 1942, there was no way to evacuate the thousands of Indians who now wanted to flee both from the Burmese and the Japs. There were, too, the small British civilian population of men, women and children. These thousands all had to be got out of Burma as best they could.

Rangoon had a very large population of Indians and they now

all travelled north. Several thousand crossed the Irrawaddy river and walked up the coastal trail by which, eventually, many reached Bengal. Others with cars drove them as far north as possible until the road ended. There they dumped the cars in great car graveyards, and then walked the rest of the way on mountain tracks via Imphal. A third lot went much further north by train. When the line ended, they too walked across the mountains, but came out in northern Assam, near Ledo.

The two northern refugee routes were helped along by the initiative of the British tea-planters in Assam who took food into the hills, and organised rest-camps on the way. Many thousands were helped by these men and their labour forces. Meanwhile, back in Assam, the planters' wives helped organise and run emergency hospitals for those sick that arrived out. But many died on that long walk across the mountains.

In the meantime, our troops were fighting a losing battle with great bravery, and under enormous difficulties and hardships. The unexpectedness and the vast number of refugees posed a very real problem for the north-east of India. Thus, when our soldiers, too, eventually trekked across the mountains, they found few preparations or reinforcements and so, instead of going to rest-camps, they had to stay put and keep guard for India.

Distances were so vast and communications so difficult, it seemed impossible for anyone in England to comprehend. I remember reading in the English papers about our Army having to evacuate from Burma but, to us then, it was just one more thing in the chain of disasters that was happening to the Allies.

In 1942, Gandhi took the opportunity to proclaim Civil Disobedience throughout India, and the Congress chiefs had to be arrested and imprisoned. Riots in Calcutta were soon stopped, but along the railways serving Calcutta and the Burma Front there was much trouble. Stations were attacked, lines ripped up, and Europeans pulled out of trains and killed. It was two or three weeks before the army got the situation in hand. However, the always possible Civil disturbances tied down large numbers of our troops unnecessarily, and made all communications to the Front more difficult.

The Monsoon rains had stopped the Japs invading further but

anyway, their communcations, too, were stretched to the limit. However there was always the threat of invasion in Calcutta, though it never happened. This, too, held down troops and slowed the building of our new offensive.

General Stilwell, of the American Army, had been made Commander of the Chinese armies under General Chiang Kai-Shek. They had been fighting the Japanese for some years and now offered their help in return for arms and supplies. These, in the past, had been sent to them by the British-built Burma road, based on Rangoon. This was now useless so two projects were started instead; the airlift, 'Over the Hump' to Chungking, and the building of a road from Ledo to connect up with the old Burma road, via Myitkyina. The transport pilots did a fine and brave job for, after refuelling at one of the air-fields in northern Assam, they then had to fly over the very high Tibetan mountains into China, and this was dangerous. They flew this route right into 1945.

The Ledo road was backed by General Stilwell, but it was a controversial issue as General Slim thought that the manpower and resources could be better employed. Eventually it was finished, but only two convoys ever went the full length of it.

British road building was concentrated on a motor road from Dimapur to Imphal and down almost to the Burma frontier, an incredible feat of engineering and upkeep made mostly by labour of Indian Pioneer Corps and men from the Indian Tea Association who organised, officered and controlled some 40,000 workers. The British offensive turned to the Arakan in South Burma, where many bloody battles were fought.

A controversial figure was General Wingate. He had raised a brigade of ordinary troops whom he trained to fight behind the Jap lines, and who soon became called 'the Chindits.' His first expedition pushed 200 miles eastwards into Japanese-held Burma, being supplied as they went by air drops. They blew up bridges and cut the railway between Mandalay and Myitkyina. Eventually, through exhaustion and difficulties of supply, they returned having lost a third of their men. They had really achieved little that couldn't soon be repaired, but what they did make was a legend. They became an inspiration to the 14th Army, who heard of how they had fought behind the Jap lines and lived to come back again.

A very great problem was health. In 1943, for every man evacuated with wounds, 120 would be brought out sick. The annual malaria rate was eighty four per cent of the whole Army. The medical establishments for the 14th Army were below those of any other of our Armies, and even what was there was below strength. When more nurses were asked for from Britain, the answer came that India must provide them itself. But Indian women didn't go in for nursing and the Indian Nursing Service grew very slowly indeed.

When Lord Mountbatten was made Supreme Commander of S.E. Asia, he backed General Slim both with the problem of health and, just as important, the prevention of disease. Much research was done on drugs, and later Penicillin, Mepacrine (to prevent malaria) and D.D.T. arrived and made an enormous difference towards the end of the war.

In the meantime, a great chain of Forward hospitals had to be built, mostly Basha huts made from bamboo. These had to be staffed and all nursing sisters were in short supply in India. Lady Mountbatten was head of St John Ambulance so the idea came – why not ask for V.A.D. nurses from the British Red Cross to work with the Indian Army? Things worked slowly and it wasn't until April 1944 that the call for volunteers came to us.

A second large batch of Chindits were flown into Northern Burma on 22nd March. They landed in several airstrips cut in the jungle, and were to help General Stilwell and his Chinese to retake northern Burma. Originally, they were only going in for two months, but Wingate was tragically killed in a flying accident so his Chindits were left under Stilwell's command. It was an extra two months before they were flown out in an exhausted condition to hospitals in northern Assam. In the meantime, the Japs had started a big offensive towards India, and cut off and besieged our troops round Imphal. A very savage battle was fought by the tiny garrison at Kohima against incredible odds. That they held out and won was the turning point of the war. If the Japs had taken Kohima, then the road was open down to Dimapur where they could have cut the railway and all Assam and

Bengal would have lain open to them. However, it was the 22nd June before General Slim said that the battle of Imphal and Kohima was won.

Now it was the 14th Army's turn to take the initiative and advance into Burma. When we V.A.D.s arrived, preparations were going on and every hospital knew how important it was to be ready for the many casualties that would follow.

1

The day our bombers started flying south instead of out to sea, we knew that the invasion of France had started. Later it was given out on the radio that our troops were invading Normandy – and all Britain held its breath.

It was June 1944, and I was on leave at home on the Essex coast, waiting for my embarkation orders for nursing in India. When the letter from the Red Cross came asking me to volunteer, I jumped at it. After all, I had been born in India, so in a way it was like going home.

At last a movement order came for me to report to London. London, wasn't that where the flying bombs were directed? For on 13th June Germany launched the new secret weapon – pilotless flying bombs and all aimed at London. They flew overhead with a buzzing noise, and were soon nicknamed Buzz-bombs, or Doodle-bugs. When their engines stopped, there was a silence, a long frightening moment while they fell, and then a great crash as they exploded on landing.

But perhaps we would be moving on straight away? After all we had been told of the urgency to be packed up and ready. So in great excitement I set off, complete with my air-tight steel trunk, and at Liverpool Street found that I was to be one of fifty V.A.D.s billeted in a Salvation Army hostel in Bloomsbury. The other 200 girls were spread out in groups around London, and all of us under strict secrecy orders, with no idea where or when we would be moving on. This was the first lesson that we learnt in that we would spend months of our time in the future just waiting around, and should never wonder at anything that happened.

While there, we heard many Doodle-bugs crash both by day and by night. One was on the Sunday when we went to Matins at Westminster Abbey and, during the sermon, a buzzing came closer and closer. The preacher paused only slightly when the crash sounded, and then carried on as calmly as before.

Another time, while crossing Trafalgar Square, we heard a bomb buzzing closer and closer. Then the engine cut out, and, running for shelter, we just had time to crouch down behind one of the big stone lions before there came the most awful explosion. I stood up and looked down Whitehall, horrified to see stones, rubble and flames shooting high in the air. I later heard that it was St Thomas's that had been hit. This shocked me as I had heard so much of this hospital from the Q.A. Army Sisters. Perhaps I might have gone to train there, but St Thomas's would never accept any girl under five foot three inches – and I was only five foot one.

When called up at the start of the War, the Doctor, who did our medical inspections, took the same poor view of my stature, and down graded me to 'B'. I was annoyed and argued with him, and eventually he gave in. "All right, then." he said. "You don't look very strong to me, but have it your own way," and he crossed out the 'B' and put 'A'. If he hadn't, I wouldn't have been allowed to go over-seas, and so would never have had this story to tell.

At last on the eighth morning we were told to be ready to leave that evening, destination unknown. However, our excitement sobered when the Salvation Army held a little service to pray for both our work and our safety. It wasn't until very late that evening that all our groups joined up on a platform in an eerily deserted King's Cross station.

There was just one train there. And it seemed only natural that the group of officers beside it should be directed to the First Class coaches, while we V.A.D.s were packed into the Third. For thirty hours we rattled along, slowing down through Edinburgh, then west to Glagow, and on along the Firth of Clyde until we stopped at a quayside. What a roundabout way we had come, but now that we could see the size of the convoy we were joining, we realised how important all that secrecy had been.

As we scrambled out, it slowly dawned on us that, over-night, we had turned into Very Important Personages. We were waved through Customs ahead of our First class travelling companions and escorted down to a tender that took us out to the S.S. Strathnaver, whose decks and rails already bulged with troops. There was a buzz of excitement and cheers as we girls drew alongside, and then we hurried up the gangway and along to our cabins.

Pre-war, the Strathnaver had been one of the stars of the P & O line, but now she was converted into a troopship. Our cabins had been First class doubles with private bathrooms. Now there were ten bunks in double rows around the walls, one hanging cupboard and a chest with half a drawer each, and our suitcases went under the bottom bunks. Heavy luggage went into the hold, but when the weather got hot we were able to go down and switch clothes for Tropical wear. The bathroom looked wonderful. It was a delight to be able to clean up, but not so good to find only sea water in the bath, and just for one hour, morning and evening, fresh water in the hand basin.

Word came round that we were to assemble at Boat Stations, which for us was on "A" deck, the very top one of all. And here Miss Corsar, our Commandant, gave instructions re meals etc. What a sight we saw around us, as the Clyde was filled with ships of every size and shape.

On going down to dinner, it all seemed unbelievable. There were bowls of sugar and slabs of butter on the tables, all for us to have as much as we wanted, a three course meal followed by coffee, and then the biggest surprise, a banana each. For in wartime England these were rationed for children only. One girl took an extra banana and gave it to the soldier on guard outside our cabins. "My God," he said. "Where did you get that?"

Afterwards we went up on deck again to see the ships, and watch all the little boats chugging around. Early to bed, but it was difficult to sleep with so much to think of, so much to say goodbye to. I had left in an excited dream. Only now did it come home to me how much, and how many people I was leaving behind.

Gradually we got moving and, under cover of darkness, slipped down the Clyde, north past Ireland, and then out into the Atlantic. Because of the blackout, portholes had to be kept closed at night, so it wasn't until next morning that we could get up on

3

deck and look around. What a fascinating sight we saw: a vast convoy of ships of all shapes and sizes, with Royal Navy destroyers shepherding us along. I never tired of watching them bobbing around, while the whole convoy kept the pace of the slowest boat.

Each morning Boat drill was the rule for everyone, while the ship's Captain made his daily inspection below. Some senior Army officers took charge of us, and one of them barked an order to "FALL IN." Well, there was a burst of laughter for none of us knew how to drill. After that the only order we ever got was, "Will you all stand in line now please?"

The officers managed to keep straight faces but under great difficulty at times. They explained to us about Boat Drill. In an emergency, all boats and rafts would be immediately lowered into the sea, and then it was up to us to jump over the side and swim to the nearest one. We were issued with Life jackets which we must never for a moment be without. They made us practise putting them on quickly, and warned, "When you jump mind you hold them down in front of you, or you will break your necks."

It was a frightening enough thought to jump from that height without being told that last order. We later heard that these officers had instructions to throw us over-board if our nerves should fail. Thank goodness it never had to happen. Just once were we woken by depth charges going off and there were no casualties among the convoy.

Gradually we got into a daily routine. On deck we were allowed to wear navy slacks and jerseys, though for all meals we had to be correctly dressed in off-duty suits. This was annoyingly tedious, but actually kept us well occupied. With ten in a cabin, it took half an hour to change both before and after each meal, what with queueing for the wash basin and mirror and then everything had to be left tidy and ship-shape.

We girls were lucky with our cabins, for the junior officers slept in rows of tiered bunks in what had been passenger lounges, while the poor men of lower ranks had to sleep below decks in converted holds. Life must have been very grim for them and desperately hot once in the Tropics. At Suez, one man who could stand it no longer threw himself overboard and drowned. The ship carried about 6,000 troops and the voyage took nearly six weeks.

We sailed right across the Atlantic to avoid enemy planes, then back East again, but when getting near Spain we circled until nightfall and then headed for Gibraltar. Lights twinkled from the mainland as we quietly slipped through the Straits and into the Mediterranean.

Next morning we found that our convoy had shrunk. Some days later, the radio reported a new invasion of our troops on the South of France, so we had given cover to these ships as they passed Spain.

The weather was mostly fine and we sat on deck on our rugs. The Ship's radio told of Flying bombs, but England seemed to be another world. Now there were sweets to buy in the canteen, also kirbigrips and hairpins, no alcohol on board, but plenty of soft drinks for sale.

We soon made friendships with the hundreds of officers who shared our decks, and 'A' deck rail was a favourite place in the evenings. We would watch the sea and the stars and laugh, while shipboard romances came and went and life was lazy and pleasant.

At long last we reached Egypt. We were the first big convoy through Suez and, as there was no stopping on the Mediterranean side, each ship passed into the Canal as soon as possible. The Captain gave orders for all ranks to keep Boat-stations as there were so many exciting things to watch. If everyone had rushed to the same side of the ship, we might have tipped over, for there was little weight below with most of the holds kept clear for sleeping accommodation. So most of the day we sat watching the amazing panorama of the desert and the gaunt, rocky outline of the Sinai mountains behind. All along the Canal, guarding it, were British troops. They waved and cheered each ship as she passed, and when they saw us girls, there was much whistling and cat-calling.

Miss Corsar now took the opportunity to call us together and gave us Headquarter's orders regarding the Tropics. Enormous topee sunhats were issued with instructions that, while on deck, we must always wear them between 9 a.m. and 5 p.m. to ward off sun-stroke. She then went on to warn us of the other great tropical danger – MEN. Hot weather could have an over-exciting effect on them, so we must all watch out and generally defend our virtue, keeping up the high standards expected of us by the Red Cross.

She was a capable and kindly Commandant whom we all liked and respected. She also had a good clear voice that carried round to the other side of the deck where groups of officers were hidden, listening with delighted attention.

They soon spread the news and that evening, from all sides, we heard "Remember girls, we men go mad to-night!" There was a romantic full moon but, crammed along the ship's rails like sardines, we couldn't be in much danger. Still it wasn't long before the men had something else to tease us about as well.

The convoy stopped at Suez for provisioning and fresh water. By now we were wearing tropical uniform and our navy blue suits had been replaced by smart-looking shirts and skirts made of nursing blue material, but of very poor quality.

Down in the dining room the heat was terrific and, coming up from second sitting of lunch next day, I heard laughter and hubbub coming from our cabin. "Whatever's happened?" I asked.

"We've all turned blue. Just like a lot of Ancient Britons, and it won't scrub off. Take your shirt off, Marian, and look."

Sure enough, when I pulled off my sweaty and dripping blouse, the colour was running out in great patches over my skin. I washed and washed but still the blue was there.

From then on we realised how inadequate much of our uniform was for the Tropics. There was one apron each, for ceremonial use only. But if no aprons, why only three dresses? How could we keep them clean for the wards? Indeed, what would they look like by the time we reached India? The thick cotton stockings already felt so hot: our white felt hats for off-duty, soon turned a nasty grey; those awful, out of date sun-topees. In fact we were soon to find that much was sadly lacking: not only our clothes, but later the camp equipment with which we were issued. An added note to our uniform list said that civilian clothes were not needed. Fortunately, I had ignored that and packed some dresses in the bottom of my trunk – surely we would have some Leave sometime? Eventually we laughed it off and gave up the unequal struggle to keep clean. For it all added to the general hilarity, what with the men going mad and the girls turning blue.

We were three days at Suez while the convoy was reprovisioned and watered. We had the luxury of fresh water all day in our basins, so there was continual washing, hair-washing etc. On deck we had so much to look at, with little boats bustling around, and at night it was like fairy-land with the lights twinkling from the shore. Now, too, the 'Black-out' was lifted and we were only 'Browned off,' which meant that we could have port-holes open, but with lights dim.

Because of the great heat, each ship, when fully provisioned, set off on her own at full speed down the Red Sea. Once at Aden, the air was cooler and the convoy waited to collect up again, before setting off sedately for Bombay.

By now, most of us girls were feeling weary, longing for dry land and, strangely enough, wanting to get down to a job of work. There were several Medical officers among the passengers, and they were told to give us lectures on Malaria and Tropical Hygiene. This was a good idea except that they had all been to the same lectures themselves so, most afternoons, the 'Life History of the Malaria Mosquito' was repeated to us by another embarrassed young doctor. Once, in the Indian Ocean, I played truant and hid in the bow of the ship. It served me right for by then the sea was quite rough. I felt sea-sick for the first time and had to escape to my cabin.

At last, on the 15th August, we arrived at Bombay, but were disappointed in our first sight of India. There was none of the Eastern magic that we were expecting, for it was not long after the big fire that had destroyed most of the dock buildings. So our view of the port reminded us of the blackened bomb-sites in the cities back in England. Still, we were delighted to disembark and find an ambulance train waiting to take us on.

In spite of being rather scruffy looking, we had dressed correctly for leaving the ship, and as it was still afternoon, we wore our large sun-topees and also beige cotton stockings. We were still wearing those topees when our train arrived at Poona at

11 p.m, that evening. I think that they caused as much of a sensation as any of our later exploits. This, too, was the last time that we wore stockings, for they cost a fantastic sum in India and no one wore them.

A fleet of station waggons waited for us with a charming W.V.S. woman in charge, and they whisked us off to our transit camp at Kirkee, a few miles out of Poona. That is – all of us except one girl who was married to a R.A.M.C. officer who had somehow managed to be there to meet her. To Miss Cörsar's dismay, he had a permit to take her straight off on leave with him, and she wasn't the only one to wonder if we would ever have her back!

Our transit camp was in an empty wing of the hospital at Kirkee, so we slept in long hospital wards with about thirty beds in each. Thick army mosquito nets hung above each bed and we were shown how to drape them round the beds and carefully tuck them in without letting one mosquito inside. We looked after ourselves without servants, which turned out to be a relief as all was so very new to us – and what a real pleasure it was to wash and iron our clothes and get really clean again! But in the dining-room we were waited on by Indian bearers, and we had to remember not to stack up the plates ourselves at the end of each meal.

After breakfast we paraded for routine Cholera and Plague injections, and then had the day in camp to get over them and settle in. Just as well as there was a very exhausting three weeks to follow.

We found that we were to be used as a big propaganda exercise to show that well-educated British girls would nurse, in the hopes of encouraging Indian and Anglo-Indian girls to follow suit. So the Governor and his wife inspected us, and all was filmed by a cinema news team. Press shots were taken and we were written up and our doings given much publicity by newspapers, including the special army paper 'S.E.A.C.' This all seemed fun at the time but it didn't make us popular with the Q.A. Army Sisters. In fact we found later that it took a lot of living down.

Miss Patterson, the Matron in Chief, India, came to inspect us. She advised us to make the most of our good times in Poona, for where we were going there would be no time for play. She told us that if we worked as hard as we had in England, then we would set a good example to show how well British girls could work. Troops usually had three to six months' acclimatisation before being sent to Forward areas. However there was such a shortage of nurses, we were all to be posted direct to the 14th Army. In the meantime we were to work in the mornings only at local British hospitals, and the rest of the time was free for three weeks of incredible gaiety.

The Governor's wife gave a Ball for us, which made a great start, and for this we wore our clean caps, aprons and dresses for the first and last time in India. We must have been a surprising sight in Government House, and we all had a wonderful time. But next morning, I found that the backs of my legs were bitten and was told·that they were Bug bites which I had probably picked up sitting on a cane chair while on a Government house verandah, as our dresses weren't long enough to protect us. This was one of the many little surprises India had in store for us.

We found that all women's services were allowed to wear mufti off-duty, so I was delighted that I had brought some dresses with me. Still, I joined the shopping spree into Poona and bought smart shoes, and even a hat for the Races. What excitement to shop without clothing coupons. We felt like children let loose in a sweet shop and, needless to say, the local shops made the most of their good fortune!

Poona is 5,000 feet up so the air was warm without being too hot. With its big Army garrison it was rather an Anglicised and suburban-looking Indian town. Still there was much to see, and most of the girls were shocked at the poverty in the Bazaar, and all exclaimed at the dirt and smell. To me, it was evocative of past happy childhood days, and even the smells brought back happy memories.

I had become friendly with Verity Iles on board ship. She had red hair, green eyes and a lovely sense of humour. Like me, she had been born in India and had spent her early childhood there so, to us, nothing seemed quite as strange as to the other girls. As children, we had been spoilt 'Missy Babas' and all Indians were our friends. The sights and sounds seemed natural, bringing back past forgotten memories and we felt at home.

Noel Coward once described a car in India as being "A horn driven at great speed." The trucks that took us in and out of Poona reminded me of this saying. The road was crowded with pedestrians, rickshaws, bicycles and, a big hazard, cows. Cows are sacred in the Hindu religion and allowed to wander where they like. So we drove into town, Toot-toot, Toot-toot, Toot-toot, in and out through the various obstacles and, amazingly, never had an accident.

We did no real nursing in the hospitals as they were all fully staffed, but at least we could talk to the men about England and their families. The need for this had been brought home to Verity and myself when one morning we missed the official transport back from Poona. We waved down a hiring-car, but then a British sergeant dashed up and, very excitedly, insisted on taking us in the car himself. We tried to refuse but, apart from making a scene in front of the small crowd that was collecting, we had to agree. To our relief he sat in front while Verity and I perched nervously at the back. He talked fast and non-stop all the way to Kirkee, of how he had been in India for four years and much of that time in fighting areas. We realised that he must be a mental case as he just went on and on and on. He told us about his wife and children and of his home in England, and soon we realised how desperately lonely he was. On arrival at Kirkee, he helped us out and said that we were the first English girls that he had spoken to for years and he thanked us for coming with him. Then he gave a smart salute and got back into the hiring-car. This man had cracked under the strain and was being repatriated home. However, there were thousands more just as lonely as him, and the odd word from us could give them pleasure.

After our hospital mornings, the rest of the day was taken up with lunches, dances, parties at local Messes and every sort of date. But always, of course, there was safety in numbers, both in groups and also the number of different escorts who took us out. On the whole we were a sensible crowd of girls, that is, all except for one girl whom I will call 'Muggins.'

There was a very good looking young Indian officer attached to the Transit camp, and Muggins fell madly in love with him. She told everyone that he had proposed and that she was going to marry him. An unlikely enough story we thought, considering that he probably had a perfectly good Indian wife back home. But on hearing this, our Commandant took the initiative. Muggins had complained of some minor ailment, probably due to a hangover, and Miss Corsar promptly whipped her into hospital with a request to the staff to keep her there. "Good for Corsar," I told the others. She had been my Commandant early on in the war and I wasn't surprised at the brilliant way she had solved the problem of Muggins!

One day I was taken to the Races, which were a popular social affair both for Europeans and Indians. There were many Indian ladies there, and we watched how gracefully they walked in their beautiful silk saris. They were mostly in little groups making lovely splashes of colour around the paddock. Much money went on betting and it highlighted the great extremes between rich and poor in India.

Our holiday ended; we had our second Plague injections, and were issued with camp equipment: camp bed, bath, basin, metal drinking water bottle and mosquito boots. The latter were the most extraordinary things: hard, pointed-toed shoes with wide canvas tops reaching right up our legs and fastened there by stocking suspenders. No one had ever seen their like before. it was as well we never had to wear them, as I later discovered that I had been issued with two left feet.

Movement orders had come through; we were now divided up into groups, and I found that I was in charge of a party of ten to go to a hospital at Panitola. No one had heard of the place and, security being so tight, no one would look it up.

A Security officer came and gave us a talk, saying that, while working in hospitals, we were bound to hear of the movement of troops. We must never, ever, talk of it. In England there had been notices warning one that "Walls have ears," but here in India it was doubly important. Perhaps that was why people in Poona seemed to know nothing of the 14th Army and the war it was fighting. Those who did, didn't speak of it. Even in Calcutta when we met so many men back from the Burma front, nobody spoke about the fighting. I never saw a map until after the War and was always confused as to where the different places were. All that we might say in letters home were that we were going to Forward hospitals on the Burma front.

Now no one was allowed out of camp, and next morning we started off again by ambulance train for Calcutta. There were just two air-conditioned coaches and, by pure luck, I picked that part of the train for our group, for which I later got much undeserved praise. We were three days and nights chugging across India by steam train, and we never stopped except for refuelling and watering the engine. Our only exercise was to walk up and down the carriages, and we soon realised how lucky we were in our air-conditioned splendour. The rest of the train was very hot indeed and, of course, smuts blew in at the windows.

Meals were served in the carriages by the train ward-boys. It was amusing to remember the lectures on Hygiene that we had suffered on board ship: eg. "When eating an orange, first wash both it and your hands, then peel it and wash your hands again before eating." The washing up arrangements on the train seemed to be done in a bowl on the floor, and the crockery spread around to dry. In spite of this we survived and I, for one, never had dysentery.

It was a tedious, uneventful journey but at least we could rest and sleep and get to know each other. While in Poona, Miss Corsar had told us all to give our preferences as to the friends with whom we would like to be posted. Her idea was that as we were going to be in strange surroundings and in outlandish places, we should each have one friend with whom we could really relax when off-duty, but, should never be in a bunch of friends together because that might cause cliques – a thoughtful and far-seeing arrangement. So I found that we were really a group of five pairs, and Verity with me. The others were the doctor's wife, also called Marian, who had safely returned from Leave with her husband, and seven others from hospitals all over England. They had all nursed for some years, but I was the only one to have been an Army Mobile V.A.D. This was perhaps why I had the dubious honour of being in charge of them – at least I would know that R.T.O. stood for Railway Transport Office, or Officer, and that they would be responsible for our travel arrangements.

The others were curious as to how I had been in the Army before. "An ex-army V.A.D. came to our hospital last Spring," said one. "She said that she had trouble getting out. What happened?"

So I explained how originally we had enlisted as civilians attached to the army, but with semi-officer status. I had been at the Cambridge hospital, Aldershot, and lucky to be there, for Matron Davies, though very strict, was a good friend to us V.A.D.s. She saw to it that we had lectures and training and, before long, most of us put up our Grade 1, brooches.

However, early in 1944, we were taken fully into the army but given the rank of privates. We felt sadly disillusioned that, after so many years of hard work, we should be demoted, with no possibility of promotion. Though there was much moral pressure on us by the Red Cross to take the new terms, many of us girls left to join civilian hospitals. I went one better for, though there was a strict labour law that we must still nurse, I found a loop-hole and got taken on in one of Bevan's new schemes, and started training as a draughtswoman.

It was a big change after being on my feet all day, not to speak of the mental strain of learning Mathematics again. I put on a stone in weight, partly the result of very good rations as I was billeted on a butcher and his wife. Incidentally this couple had slipped the Billeting officer a joint of beef in exchange for a 'nice quiet girl', and I was the exchange.

But there was continual news of preparations going on for the invasion of France, and I sometimes regretted giving up nursing. The time was coming when every single nurse would be needed and I wouldn't be there. Then suddenly a letter arrived from the Red Cross asking me to volunteer again as a V.A.D., but with officer status in the Indian army. I went up to Headquarters in London to be interviewed by a Board and they asked me about my new work.

"When I first got your letter," I answered, "I showed it to my Instructor. He said that if I stayed on I would make a success of the course, but he would put nothing in my way if I wanted to leave."

At that, I heard some approving murmurs around and, later, an official said to me, "That was a wonderful wangle you did getting out of nursing like that. However did you manage it?"

"So you see," I ended, "Not everyone at H.Q. disapproved of us leaving the army, for they passed me for India straight away."

Further along the coach I had spotted Muggins. At first she complained bitterly, "If I was so ill that I had to be in hospital, why am I well enough to travel now?" But by the end of the journey she seemed to be more regretful of the parties that she had missed than of her handsome ex-fiance! I was certainly thankful that she wasn't one of my little group.

2

We were nearing Calcutta but had seen little as, for the last thirty six hours, we had been told to keep the train blinds down both by day and by night. Our numbers were again divided with the largest group to go on river boats to their hospitals. The rest of us were split up in Calcutta and we ten were included in the forty booked into the Grand Hotel, which had been converted into an officers' hostel.

Having been cocooned in our coaches for the last three days, we then disembarked into the seething turmoil of Howrah station, where there seemed to be as many onlookers as travellers, and all the time a great shouting and talking. Up till now we had had Miss Corsar to look after us; from now on we were on our own, so we made our way out to some waiting lorries which whisked us off at great speed through the bazaars and into central Calcutta.

It was a big change from Poona. There were thousands and thousands of people thronging the sidewalks, while whole families lay or squatted by the walls. There was much talking, jostling, and everything so very smelly and dirty. Above all there was the awful poverty. Calcutta had always had a huge population but, since the Burmese war, there had been so many refugees. With the army there too, the place seemed bursting at the seams.

The Grand is in Chowringee, a wide road facing the Maidan – or big public park. Here at least there seemed more space until, on going into the hotel we found it just as crowded. For inside it was full of officers on Leave, and our arrival caused a sensation. As we queued at the office to book in, there was a second queue along beside us trying to talk, ask questions, make dates, and so it went on for the whole of our stay. It was bad enough looking after myself, without nine others, and I soon found that I would be losing Verity.

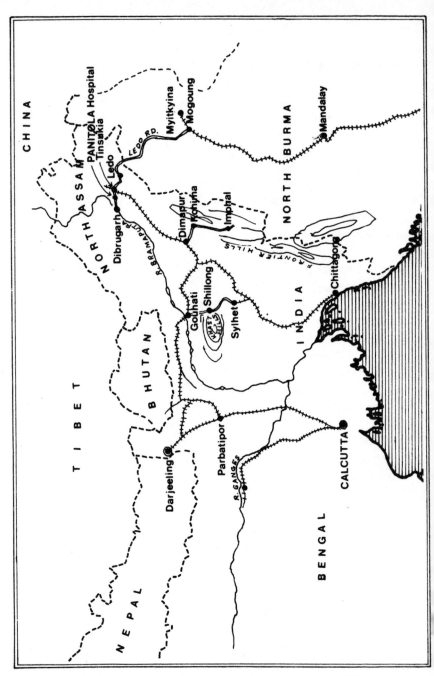

The map of India and Burma in 1944 showing the route to and from Dibrugarh and Panitola Hospital.

16

"Marian," she called rushing up to me. "Do you remember that I told you of an old friend of mine who is a Gurkha officer somewhere in the 14th Army? Well, I've just met him, for he is here now in the hall. Come and see," urged Verity in great excitement.

She introduced me to Peter, a major of only 24 years, wearing shabby jungle green battle-dress. "This is just too marvellous," he said. "I'd heard that Verity was coming out here, so when I read in a S.E.A.C. paper that V.A.D.s had arrived in Poona, I asked for two weeks' leave from my colonel. I flew down to Calcutta this morning and came to the Grand to change, before catching a train on. Then I saw some nurses and they found Verity for me. It's almost unbelievable."

"Yes, and he's asked me to stay on in Calcutta. Do you think that would be possible?"

What could I say but, "Yes, so long as you get permission from someone at H.Q. here."

So off they went to the Fort, where they told their tale to a senior staff officer. He must have looked at their two young faces and their anxious eyes: the young man on leave from a fighting area, and the girl fresh out from England. He was only human, and the red tape in him melted away. "Let me see," he said turning to Verity, "What relation is he to you? He can't be your brother as he has a different surname. Perhaps he is your step-brother?"

To this they both delightedly agreed, and thanked him gratefully. On the way back they called in at the Lady Mary Herbert hostel, the local Y.W.C.A. for women's services, and reserved a bed for Verity to stay there for one week. Then back they came in triumph and handed me the written permission for "V.A.D. Iles to have one week's Compassionate Leave."

There was an R.T.O. at the Grand who was to make our travelling arrangements, but he didn't have much idea of what, or where, Panitola was, and so he promised to make enquiries and let me know. In the meantime we split up into the two five bedded rooms that were allotted us, and then were entertained downstairs by the crowds below – that is, after I had arranged for them to all check with me three times a day.

That evening, a trio of R.A.F. officers asked me to join them for dinner and I accepted as one of them actually knew where Panitola was. He couldn't draw any maps or give much explanation, but said that he thought it was right up in the north of Assam. "There's a hospital near the airfield where we refuel before flying over the mountains to China. If so, it will take you several days travel before you get there. You'll have to cross the Brahmaputra river so that means at least two changes of trains."

The three men saw my eyes widen in alarm, and then they all warmed to it with questions and horrifying tales. "Do you mean that you girls have only been in India a month? Can you speak Urdu? Well then, how are you going to cope with the porters?"

"But the R.T.O. will look after us," I answered.

At this they all laughed. "Will an R.T.O. travel with you? Have you ever travelled in a train in India by yourselves, before?

"I wouldn't go on that journey for anything. I would rather fly into Burma anyday."

"The RAF would never let their nurses travel unescorted."

"They must be mad to let you loose on that railway. You know that it's been taken over by the Army and is chaotic east of the river."

"Remember train thieves are incredibly clever. A chap I know woke up in the morning to find that all his luggage and clothes had gone, and he hadn't heard a thing."

"Take some sandwiches with you and fill your water bottles, and make sure that it is drinking water too. You don't want to end up with dysentery."

I realised that they were RAF types who were probably teasing me, while getting in digs at the Army at the same time. Still it was worth listening to them, and I would take their advice about food and water.

Later that evening Freda burst into our room, "I've just met a rat in the passage."

"He's not following you in here, is he?" I asked.

"No, it was a real live animal rat. It scuttled past me and didn't bother about my being there," she said with real horror in her voice. After all that I had been hearing that evening, I felt that we might all meet worse things than a brown rat. I didn't say much about it to the other girls, for it still surprised me the way they took my leadership for granted. I suppose that we all felt so lost and strange, that they in their innocence relied on me, just as I did on the R.T.O.

It wasn't until our second evening that the R.T.O. told me that we were to leave the next morning for a station called Tinsukia. He also told me how lucky we were that he had reserved us seats on the Assam Mail, and so we would travel in great comfort. "Have all your baggage ready by 12 noon and a lorry will take it to Howrah station. All you have to do is to follow, and the station R.T.O. will embark you there." How easy he made it sound!

Peter was so grateful to me for allowing Verity to stay behind, that he offered to see us off next day, and I was certainly thankful for his help. For we each had four pieces of luggage comprising one small tin trunk, one large suitcase, a valise for our bedding roll, and· a big canvas bag of camp equipment. So, as we were taking Verity's as well; that meant forty pieces, and thirty or forty porters were needed at each station. No trolleys were used, for each man would put a pad of cloth on his head, and then balance a box on top of it.

At 10 a.m. we started collecting the baggage. I only knew two words of Urdu, one was "Go" and the other "Come". So I found the luggage pieces and said "Jau" to a porter who would then take it out to Peter who was collecting them all on the pavement outside. It was very, very, hot and the noise terrible, with all the porters shouting at once – or so it seemed to me. Verity kept us going with glasses of orange juice, and by 11.45 everything was in the waiting lorry. Peter said that he would travel with the baggage and see it into the train, while we followed in a second lorry.

Not until we were leaving did the R.T.O. say, "Be sure to catch the train as your beds are all taken here tonight. The twenty girls who left yesterday missed it, and had to travel on a slow one later. Oh, and watch out for the driver. He's a bit wild, so perhaps you had better sit in front to keep an eye on him," he added to me as an afterthought.

Our driver knew only one speed – fast. We raced through Calcutta and its crowded bazaars and, with a screech of brakes, bang into a car. Fortunately it was empty, but a crowd started to collect, and the driver looked at me to ask what to do?

Inspiration came: "Jau," I yelled. He backed and was away, leaving a policeman hastily writing down his number.

Thankfully we arrived at the station only to find a distraught-looking Peter waving from the pavement. "It's no good," he said. "You'll never catch the train. The R.T.O. hasn't heard of you and they won't let me move the luggage."

"We must, we must," I wailed. "I could never go through another morning like this one. You look after everything while I go to the R.T.O." Desperation gave me courage and fire in my eye, and I dashed to the Transport office and demanded to see who was in charge there.

The American officer looked under my enormous sun topee at the five foot one inch of furious indignation. "I am sorry about this, Sister. I'd never heard of V.A.D.s before and I thought you were some new sort of soldier. We've booked you on a troop train, which Nurses aren't allowed to travel on. However I'll try and get things fixed. ."

Fifteen minutes to go and forty pieces of luggage to get through what looked like pandemonium at the station. A sergeant rushed us along and found one empty carriage at the end of the train. Peter, meanwhile, manfully organised a stream of porters to the guardsvan. All were in at last, as, a minute later, the whistle blew and we were off. The last sight of him was of a noble figure tipping a long line of men, which was rapidly growing as every porter in the station rushed to join on.

We sank back on our wooden seats and took stock of the carriage that we were in: Third class, with two wooden benches running down each side, and a little lavatory at one end. From the smell alone, we knew it must be one and, "Oh dear," someone said. "What about the Hygiene lectures?" This then was our comfortable journey on the Assam Mail and, for all I knew, we had forty-eight hours of it. Reaction set in and I was trembling and near to tears, but someone handed me a cigarette and soon I felt better. I had told everyone to take sandwiches and fill their water bottles so at least we had something, and we drank straight from our bottles and nibbled some food as, slowly, we jogged through the Bengal countryside. Our box of a carriage got hotter and hotter and the smell worse and worse, when suddenly an

Indian bearer's face appeared at the open window. "Restaurant car open. Come next station," he said.

We gazed, astonished. We'd been warned about train thieves; would he be one? He then disappeared, hand over hand back along the train. Soon we arrived at a station and on walking up the platform found, to our delight, there was a Buffet car in front. Quickly we split into two parties and took it in turns to go there and eat, and enjoy the lovely comfort of fans and a cool dining room. We stopped at every station and so were able to run back and forth along the platform.

So far we had seen no other English people on the train, and the thought of coping with the next move and all the luggage quite appalled me. "What we need," I said, "are some men to help us. I think that we change trains this evening at the junction for Darjeeling, so perhaps some British troops will join us there."

About 11 p.m. we drew in to Parbatipur, and were soon surrounded by a shouting crowd of porters. But then, oh joy! There were an English R.T.O. and two smiling sergeants carrying hot mugs of tea and a great basket of fruit. "I had a signal about you from Calcutta," said the R.T.O., "And we thought you might like some refreshments." How kind and cheering they were and, what was more, they had even heard of Panitola, but even they were a bit vague as to when we should arrive.

Just then Diane nudged me, "See what I see?" For there further along the platform was a little group of jungle green clad officers.

"All right," I said. "We depend on you, Diane." They had three first class carriages reserved for us with comfortable, padded sleeping bunks, and also good clean W.C.s with water that actually ran from the taps. They told us that we could sleep until morning when we would change again to cross the Brahmaputra and, finally, they locked us all safely in.

Dorothy and Nancy had a carriage to themselves. They spread their valises out and changed into pyjamas. Dorothy hung her dressing gown on the hook just above her bunk, and then they were soon asleep. Suddenly she woke up, feeling something had brushed across her face. She sat up with a scream as, just then, the train drew into a station. Nancy woke up and joined her screams with Dorothy's and, not finding the light switch, they banged on the door to be let out. People on the platform heard them and joined in the uproar with shouts and yells. At last someone managed to unlock the door. There were no thieves to be seen; just two embarrassed-looking girls. Dorothy looked round and there, on the floor, was her dressing gown. It must have brushed her face as it fell – and that was her train thief.

Morning came and we dressed ready for the next change. On arrival, Jean stayed with me to help with the luggage while the others went on ahead to the ferry boat. The usual mob of shouting porters gathered but this time the station master, himself, arrived to help. He was armed with a long whip which he cracked and didn't hesitate to use on an unauthorised man who had mixed in with the others. At last a long line of porters, each balancing a box on his head, wound its way out of the station and on to the boat.

Jean and I walked up the gangway and saw the wonderful, cheerful sight of our party of V.A.D.s and the group of Army officers, settling down to a good meal of bacon and eggs. Afterwards, a press photographer appeared and took our photos for S.E.A.C. newspaper. "V.A.D.s over the Brahmaputra," was to be the caption, I think. What a good meal, and what a happy one.

At the other side of the very wide river we were met by both a colonel and a major from the hospital at Gauhati, and they told us the sad tale of the twenty V.A.D.s who had set off the day before us. At Calcutta there had been the same muddle over their reservations, so that they missed the Mail train and had to travel on a much slower one. They had no food for thirty six hours and arrived both exhausted and frightened. They lost all their luggage and were now in Transit camp where they would stay to recover and be sorted out. So the R.A.F. were right in warning me, but even they hadn't described such an awful journey as those poor girls had. I thanked heavens that I had made such an all out effort to get on the Assam Mail.

That is why two such senior officers came to meet us, for if we hadn't arrived, they would have created hell at the R.T. office. They were relieved to see us and were wonderfully kind and helpful, taking us to our new train and dealing with the luggage and porters, and finally they found some officers going our way and asked them to take charge of us.

We were now in the Forward area where the railway had been taken over by the army, and our three first class carriages had been stripped. No seat paddings, electric light bulbs, or water in the lavatories, but our luggage was stacked in our own carriages and none of us had lost a thing. There would be another twenty hours travelling but no more changes. So what did it matter if there was no electricity, or water to wash with, for now at last the army had taken charge of us, and all seemed well with the world.

"Will you all meet us in the Buffet car for lunch?" asked one of our appointed escorts, and so it was arranged. It turned out that they were a party who had spent a sad Leave at Darjeeling, just drifting from bar to bar. They had all been out for two years at least and·on fighting fronts most of the time, so it was a thrill for them to talk to girls from England. We talked all day and they were very interested listeners to our adventures since we had arrived in India. They were also very indignant that we had been thrown into the Forward areas without any advice or training. As usual, they thought our topees hilarious and advised us to get rid of them straight away. British people no longer wore them, and certainly not the troops. So, joyfully, we threw them out of the train windows. We heard too, that for anti-malaria precautions, it was a Command order that all ranks must wear long sleeves and slacks after 6 p.m. We told them about our mosquito boots and they just fell about laughing. We had a lovely day and, of course, they paid for all our meals, and I even ended up winning nine rupees on Liar dice.

After tea, we went back to our carriages and changed into the navy slacks we had worn on board ship, warm, but not too bad by the evening. We spread out our bed-rolls ready for the night and, armed with torches, returned to the Buffet car. What a wonderful time we had, and the men said that it was the best part of their whole Leave. They all had to get off at Dimapur where they were to travel by road up to Imphal and be ready for the big Push that was coming later. Goodbyes were sad and, in some cases, really affectionate, and many addresses were exchanged. We went to our carriages, felt our way to our bed-rolls and fell into exhausted sleep.

At daybreak we were up. Miss Corsar had given instructions to arrive correctly dressed, clean and tidy. We tried our best, putting on our navy blue uniform caps but looked woefully crumpled and dirty after two days and nights without washing. What a joy, though, to think that we were arriving. Talking of the lovely breakfast we would have in the Sisters' Mess, we strode along the platform and, with triumph, I led the way into the R.T.O.s office.

He looked up, stared, and said, "Good gracious, what are you doing here? No one's expecting you for another two days!"

3

The Buffet car had been taken off the train the evening before, at Dimapur, but they had refilled our water bottles with fresh boiled water, and given us a packet of sandwiches each. So, while waiting for transport, we sat and ate our breakfast and the R.T.O. told us a bit about the hospital. He said that we were in the very north of Assam and not far from the Tibetan frontier, however we were lucky as "Panitola is the best little hospital in the Forward area." It had been converted from a tea estate hospital, for this was a great tea growing area, and was about five miles down the road towards Dibrugarh, the capital of Northern Assam. As we saw later from the ambulance that fetched us, it was a long, long, straight dirt road, full of pot-holes, while on each side stretched acres and acres of dark green bushes which, we were told, were Tea-gardens.

The Sisters' Mess was in a large field, or compound as it was called. It consisted of long huts built of plywood with thatched roofs and wide verandahs to keep out the sun. Each hut had five rooms with lean-to bathrooms behind, but the main dining room and Mess was in a hut of its own. We ten girls had one of these huts to ourselves, two to a room, and I took one for Verity and myself. The whole place was surrounded by barbed wire, and two sepoy soldiers were on guard duty at the gates both by day and by night.

A cheerful looking Sister greeted us, telling us her name was Baptie, and that she would show us around and help us to settle in. We had proper beds, made of wooden frames with lattice work threaded in between, and mosquito nets hanging from wires above. The rooms were well furnished with a hanging cupboard, a chest of drawers and two chairs. The floors were of concrete and, in the bathroom, on a slope with a hole in the side so that water could be tipped out and drain away. Our camp baths were opened out, also the basin and canvas pail at the ready. At one side was the earth closet, or 'Thunderbox'. This was a wooden seat with a pail inside which was changed twice daily by the Sweeper.

Sister Baptie explained kindly and patiently about it all as we none of us knew the language or, just as important, anything of the Indian customs. She told us that we had three servants to look after us, not that there was enough work, but none of them would do the work of others. That is where the Caste system came in, and we had to stick by it as it was a part of the Hindu religion.

I think she was aghast as to how ignorant we were and must have told Matron so. Poor Matron, she had lost seven trained Sisters to be replaced by the ten of us. When I went to report our arrival and said that one of us was on a week's Leave, she looked definitely gloomy and, on reading about the 'step-brother,' distinctly sceptical. Matron was no fool.

When we changed at tea-time into navy, woollen slacks and white shirts, she exploded. To think that we had spent three weeks in Poona, and no one had told us anything. What was the use of having lectures about malaria if we didn't have the clothes to guard against mosquitoes? We had been given part-time work in hospitals in Poona, but they had no idea about conditions in hospitals in forward areas with the 14th Army. Poona was a completely different world. People didn't forget to tell us. They just didn't know. "Well, you'd better have tomorrow off and get yourselves kitted out properly," she said dismissing us.

So, next day, we went off by ambulance to the Officers' Shop at Makum, where we brought khaki material and also other very necessary things like an umbrella and a hurricane lamp each. Then back to the Panitola tailor, who lived in a row of little bazaar shops in the village. He was an old man with a long white beard, who wore a loin cloth and sat cross-legged under a sign that said "Military Tailor". He must have collected all his friends and relations to help with the rush of work and, by next day, we all had one pair of slacks each to go on duty at 5 p.m. Soon we also had two shirts and slacks each, and later had off-duty bush shirts made and a simple khaki skirt for off-duty day wear.

We ranked as Honorary Officers and messed with the Queen Alexandra Army Sisters who must have been both curious and amused by our ignorance. A few of them enjoyed telling us the worst about everything.

"Just wait till the rains start and your shoes go mouldy."

"You have to put everything out to air in the sun at least every month, and make sure that nothing gets pinched."

"You know that there's no hairdresser up here, so don't expect to get your hair cut for at least a year," said one Sister with her hair hanging over her shoulders.

"You'll be bound to get malaria. Everyone does in this hospital – and dysentery to."

"You'll soon get tired of bully beef seven days a week."

"Watch out for snakes, scorpions, leeches, spiders."

You name it they thought of it, and so on and so on.

They weren't all like that. Sister Baptie explained to me later that they had all been looking forward to our arrival – until S.E.A.C. newspapers started promoting us. They then soon got fed up with seeing our photos and reading of our doings and, feeling pretty sour about us, decided that we needed taking down a peg. Why should the papers make such a fuss of us, when no one had bothered about them?

Besides, there was that tactless remark Lord Louis had made. Some weeks earlier he had been to inspect another hospital in the area. At the finish he turned to Matron and said, "Well that is all very efficient, but what you need now are some pretty girls. I'll be sending you up some V.A.D.s very soon." He must have meant it as a jovial aside, but the story went that Matron took it seriously, and the news soon spread through the Sisters' messes around. If Lord Louis had tried, he really couldn't have thought of anything that would give us more instant unpopularity among the Q.A. Army Sisters!

So, life seemed depressing; perhaps we did need putting in our places. Now most of us felt determined to show just how well we could cope and we would try our very best. However, these Sisters had been through a very hard time. None of them had had leave for at least a year. Some of them had been nursing at Imphal and evacuated only just in time before the siege started and, with only half an hour's notice to pack up. Panitola hospital was half empty now but they had been working flat out before, with Chindit casualties being flown out from North Burma. So, looking back, I think that they must have been a fine bunch of women, and in fact, really good nurses. But it was not until the expected rush of fresh casualties came in that we V.A.D.s became accepted, and then formed a mutual liking and respect for each other.

Next morning, we went on duty at 8 a.m. The hospital was across the road and spread over several acres of grassland. The wards were long huts, mostly built of bamboo and with thatched roofs and wide verandahs to keep out the sun. They were well spaced out, but with concrete pathways joining them and also covered by wooden roofs. The latter were necessary as, when it rained, it really rained. The monsoon was nearly over, but in between the rainy days, it was very hot and humid.

The ground around was grassed and kept fairly short by cattle grazing over it. Once I took a short cut across and a leech fastened on and bit me. It was the first leech I had seen, and it seemed so absolutely loathsome and frightening as it swelled up sucking my blood. An orderly came to my rescue and soon burnt it off with the tip of a cigarette. "Lucky it didn't get any higher, eh Nurse," he said. I never took short cuts again.

Behind the wards were the latrines. I never saw inside one as Sisters weren't allowed in and they were the M.Os responsibility for cleanliness. We had heard of so many bad things, so this was definitely a Plus. No more emptying bedpans, and no more scrubbing out bloody, or soiled sheets.

The hospital was called "Combined" as it was for both British and Indian troops. The colonel, and most of the medical officers were Indian, while the Sisters and ourselves were English. On the British wards there were R.A.M.C. orderlies, and on the Indian side nursing sepoys. On each ward was a staff of servants to do the different kinds of work. This was decreed by the "caste" that they were born in, and nothing could change that fact. Caste was almost part of the Hindu religion and we had to respect this and learn who was allowed to do what.

The wardboy dealt out the food and washed up afterwards. The pani-wallah heated water in a boiler outside and carried it around for patients' washings. However, he would not wash up dishes. The sweeper swept, or washed the floors, looked after the latrines and gave bedpans. British orderlies, sisters and nurses would give bedpans and bottles to really sick patients but NOTHING would induce a nursing sepoy to give a bedpan, even if the patient was dying. Nor were we allowed to tell them to do so.

On Indian wards, the system was complicated by having both Mohammedan and Hindu patients in the same wards. So they had to have separate meal carriers and separate cooks and kitchens. In theory, fighting troops had been absolved from these caste laws but, in practice, they were very important indeed. We white Christians were casteless in their eyes so we could never touch their food or drink. This meant that on giving them medicine, one must not touch their mouths with the glass. The patients just opened their mouths, and the medicine poured straight down.

I was lucky to go straight on to the British Surgical wards, and have time to settle in and learn a little of the language, for in a few days, Matron warned me that I would be going on to night duty at the end of the following week. Five of the V.A.D.s were on Indian wards where no one could speak English except the Sisters, but they muddled through and had a lot to tell us when they came off duty.

On my ward was one Sister, plus one or two orderlies. The patients had mainly only minor injuries, so would return to their units, but nearly all of them had jungle sores on their bodies. They all needed treatment and, above all, good food. Some of them suffered from what was called "jungle nerves". One man woke one afternoon with a terrified yell as he had seen the trees outside and thought he was back in the jungle, so we turned his bed away from the windows. Those back in India had no idea what the troops had to put up with. The fighting wasn't all, it was the existing as well, with the continuous bully beef, flies and insects. The worst part was their feeling of loneliness and the idea that they were forgotten. Even we were depressed at times with the immense distances and at being cut off from our friends. If we felt lonely, then what did those men feel like?

Discipline, or the lack of it, surprised us as everything was so different from strict hospitals in England. We sensed a "Them" and "Us" attitude in the staff. All ranks who had been out for some years had a mutual camaraderie. They were naturally wary of us and showed that we were newcomers and we still had to work to earn their respect. I watched astonished as an orderly strolled up and sat on Sister's desk while talking to her. If any of us had dared to do that back in England, we would soon have been given an unpleasant job to do. However, as we learnt later, when there was work to do everyone knew their place and jumped to it.

The hospital generated its own electricity, supplying both the Officers' and Sisters' messes as well, and I don't think it ever let us down. However, the plugs could be dangerous and liable to give one electric shocks. On my first day, while plugging in a kettle, I got a shock which both stopped my watch and burnt my hand. The latter was a nuisance as it meant a dressing and wearing a glove, which made me rather useless for doing patients' dressings. From then on, I always used a rubber glove when plugging in anything and we learned to turn on our bedroom light switch with a wooden coathanger. People said that it was to do with the damp in the air, and we just got used to it.

At 4 p.m, or 5 p.m, according to duties, we went to our rooms and shouted "Garrum pani" – or hot water. After some time, the water carrier arrived with a canvas bucket of warm water which he poured into our camp baths and then the bearer announced that the bath was ready. This, of course, meant sitting cross-legged and rinsing ourselves with a mug. Finally, we washed our undies in the same water. Then we dressed in shirt and slacks, a quick comb of the hair, and off to Mess for tea. It felt funny going on duty without a cap on one's head but we soon got used to it, just as we did at not wearing aprons over our dresses during the day, also having to make each dress last for a week. Apart from only having three dresses, we were only allowed to send six articles to the dhobi, or washerman, each week, and this included bed linen and towels. There was no starch so our caps looked limp, sorry sights by the end of a week.

I was delighted when five days later, and seven days after she had been given a week's leave, Verity and Peter arrived back.

Peter still had some days leave so he fixed himself up in a local mess, and we were able to entertain him in ours by day. They had become engaged and were wonderfully happy. They had known each other since childhood and it was a fairy story the way they had met again, and fallen in love. Verity and he spent a lot of her off-duty walking in the Tea Estate that surrounded us and we all felt better for their happiness.

Peter also busied himself finding a private bearer for us. Sisters' Messes were known to have the worst of the servants and we, as V.A.D.s had the dregs. He was going to have his future wife looked after properly and must have used his considerable charm on our "Home Sister" to allow him to change her domestic arrangements. He found us a bearer and lectured both him and the other servants on working and treating us properly. He must have put·the fear of death into them for, from then on, there was a subtle change in their attitude towards us. Verity, and I and two others shared this bearer and his monthly wages, and he certainly made life easier for us, and he also seemed really honest. We never lost any of our possessions. He would put them out to air when the sun shone, and bring them all safely in again. This helped the others as well, as the official bearer now only had the six of them to look after. It was a sad parting when Peter left but he had got Verity's promise that they would get married on his next leave. For the present, he had to return to his unit at Kohima.

Panitola hospital had seemed very strange to me, but it was doubly so for the others. None of them had been in a Military Hospital before so didn't know about army ways. Their civilian hospitals hadn't bothered to give them lectures, and few had had much training or responsibility. Years later, Verity told me of her unforgettable first day on duty. Doubtless most of the others had had as difficult a time.

Matron put her on the Indian Dysentery ward, with just one Sister and an Indian staff of nursing sepoys who could speak no English. Verity had learnt little nursing in England, and had done more housework than anything else. Now, suddenly she had to take on the work of a staff nurse. One of her first jobs was to give the Emmetine injections, and she had to admit that she had never given an injection before.

"Well, you had better learn then, hadn't you?" retorted the Sister.

Soon there were twenty patients lined up, and after being shown the first injection, she had to do the rest herself.

Verity said, "I must have hurt them for my hand was shaking, and by the end I was quivering like a jelly. But they were all so kind and brave and didn't make a sound. We had more responsibility than one could possibly have imagined. There was a Q.A. and a V.A.D. on each ward, and when Sister was off-duty, there I was in charge. The evening duty was the worst, with those shiny, black beetles that climbed up the walls, and then fell down with a plopping sound. The jackals too, when they howled outside, sounded very weird. It was quite frightening really, how much was expected of us. But always I found the nursing sepoys so kind and helpful."

I was thankful to have had the limited training and responsibility that I had in Aldershot. I first realised the difference when a Sister asked me, "Nurse, where did you learn to write such a good report?"

I was surprised, and asked her what made her think so. "Well, you are the only one among you who uses the word 'appeared'."

We had it drummed into us at the Cambridge that only trained staff might write their own opinions in reports. Untrained staff had to write that a patient 'appeared' ill – in pain – better – and so on. So that one little word may have marked me out to Matron as the first V.A.D. to be launched on night-duty, and my strange time was soon to come.

It must have been very worrying for Matron. The hospital had been warned to be ready for casualties arriving in the near future. There was little time to train us, and all she could do was throw us in at the deep end and hope for the best. To her relief – and probable surprise – she got the best from us, and somehow we managed.

As most of the Chindits had left, the hospital was only half full and the work load very easy. The Sisters were making the most of this slack time, and there were parties around in which we joined. The third evening after our arrival there was the monthly British

Other Ranks dance at Dibrugarh to which we were all taken by lorry. They were always great fun though absolutely exhausting. The men vastly outnumbered us, so that we were being constantly "excused me". Each partner would put in as many steps as he knew and we would be swung in and out and round about, until we were about dropping with tiredness. We all enjoyed ourselves, though I know that I spent the next days off-duty in bed.

One evening, the local brigadier had a party in his Mess and we all went along. After dinner, Matron said that she would like to go to the Ladies and who would go with her? The Sisters all hastily said "no", so she turned to us nurses. It seemed quite a simple enough thing to agree to, so like a Muggins, I went. The junior officer was ordered to escort us and I soon saw why the sisters had all refused. Our escort had a hurricane lamp and led the way to a bamboo-walled earth closet in the middle of the field. Matron took the lamp in with her while I made nervous conversation with the subaltern, trying to hide the noises from within. Matron then came out and we exchanged positions, and the process was repeated. After this we all three walked solemnly back again.

All I remember of that party was that the army was right. One must never, ever, volunteer for anything. Penny, on the other hand, came home very happy and excited. She thought the adjutant was absolutely wonderful and, what's more, he had asked her for a date.

Another evening, the local Gurkha Unit held a Puja festival party, to which the Sisters took four of us along with them. We sat in the front among the officers, and there were row upon row of dark faces behind. We watched the graceful rhythmic dancing of the Gurkha dancers – men dressed as women – jiggly steps and many arm and hand movements. Drink and food was passed around and the party livened up considerably. Then the dancers pulled their own officers out to dance with them in turn, followed by the rest of us, beginning with the brigadier, who gave a surprisingly good exhibition. It was a terrible moment when I was pulled out on the floor – just me and one dancer giving a duet. I must have had a good few drinks or I couldn't have done it.

A doctor from a neighbouring unit came and introduced himself and talked to me. then he said, "Come and meet my friend Peter." To my amazement Peter was a young lawyer from my village at home. What a treat it was to see his beaming face and be reminded of things in England. Last time that we had met was a little before the war when we were both acting in the local drama group in "Iolanthe." We had danced as partners, and now here we were, five years later, dancing at a Gurkha festival at the other side of the world! Peter had married a sweet girl and had a small son whom he was longing to see. I was glad to be able to send back messages about him via my mother.

Peter Church was on the staff at Sub Area HQ and they were wonderfully kind in inviting us to dinners and parties. In fact, we thought they helped us with our "censor crisis", and that was a crisis. As we were only unofficial officers, we knew that our letters were censored, but imagined the censoring was done in some office in the heart of India. But, soon after our arrival, Matron returned a letter to Diane that she had written to a boy friend back in India, saying that she must not write like that, as it would be bad for morale. Evidently she had rather gone on about things and how awful everything was, and it was so muddy. The rest of us felt furious with Diane for letting us down so, by grumbling, but also grateful that she had found out the facts about the Censor. Matron was the Censor. Every letter we wrote, she read and we wondered about the awful things we might ourselves have written.

I wrote straight off to Miss Corsar putting it, as tactfully as I could, that it was such a beastly job for poor Matron to have to do. She wrote back to say that she would approach HQ about it but, by the time her letter had arrived, either we, or Matron, had had it changed ourselves. Personally I thought it was fixed by our own H.Q.

Peter Church had asked us over to a party in his Mess at which we told everyone the story of our censored letters, and our hosts' faces were a study. We could see them thinking, "My God, their Matron will read descriptions of us and our party!" Very soon after that a Command Order came through to say that V.A.D.s were to censor their own letters – as did the Q.A. Sisters. Matron, too, must have been glad of this.

4

The next evening I went on to night duty. Only for two weeks as, because of the climate, it was particularly tiring. But it certainly was a night duty like none that I had ever experienced before. I almost felt like 'Alice in Wonderland,' never knowing what would happen next, nor what I would find in the next ward.

There was one Night-Sister, Sister Shipton, for the whole hospital, and I was her assistant and companion combined. As it was a 600 bedded hospital we had quite a lot of ground to cover, quite literally, as the wards were well separated in case of fire. I couldn't have been on with a kinder or more conscientious young woman, for she tried her best to explain things and to teach me enough Urdu to make myself understood, and never once was she impatient.

While Sister took reports from the wards, my evening started by going back to my Surgical ward to help the orderly settle the patients down for the night. There was one dangerously ill man who was my especial charge, Gunner White, who had fought with the Chindits and had bayonet wounds in his lungs. He was incredibly brave and I think the most stoical patient I had ever known. Never once did I hear him complain, and he just liked to talk of his wife and family in England. While he was in hospital, news came through that he had been awarded the Military Medal, for which I tried to congratulate him, but he wouldn't have it. All he said was that there were many others who deserved the medal as much as, or more, than himself. The surgeon had started him on a new wonder drug called Penicillin and he was the first patient in the hospital to have it. We all so hoped that it would be as miraculous as forecast. Sadly, though, it was too late, and by the time I went on night-duty he was a very ill man indeed.

Sister would then collect me and we would do the round of

36

the whole hospital. She would point out the seriously ill patients and how best to keep an eye on them. There was a night orderly on each of the British wards, and they were responsible, and gave out medicines to all on the list. If they were worried about anything, then they called the Sister. On the Indian wards, there were nursing sepoys. They had not had the same training, nor could they be trusted not to sleep at night. This surprised me but she explained that they didn't have the same chance to sleep during the day, as the Indian Lines were very noisy. I wouldn't have thought that this would have mattered as the Indian patients seemed to sleep through everything. In one ward, the nursing sepoy called Dan Singh, sang to himself in a dirge-like voice all night. I never discovered if it was to keep himself awake, or to frighten away devils.

On the Indian wards, we would be joined by the nursing sepoy carrying a basket full of the more usual medicines, plus one metal medicine glass. Sister would pour the medicine out and then poise it over the patient, who opened his mouth and down it went in one go. Sulphonomide tablets had to be very carefully watched and handed out, as they were much prized in the bazaar, where they fetched one rupee each on the Black Market. The more unpleasant the medicine tasted, the better the Indian patients thought it must be. There were two harmless bottles, one for coughs and the other for stomach pains, and they both tasted quite awful. But they were the most popular, and a good dose of one of them would ensure a night's sleep for the recipient, the patient having first rubbed his stomach or chest to show which medicine he needed.

I soon had a small but very useful vocabulary of words which, by different tones of voice, could mean different things. "Thik hai," or "All right", could be used either as a statement or a question, and was popular with the British troops as well.

During the first evening round, the noise was appalling: Convalescents singing and chattering away, while the iller ones moaned and groaned for our attention, and the nursing sepoys shouted and made more noise than anyone. Later on they would settle down, just a few groaners – with the nursing sepoys, some of whom were very good nurses while others believed in the survival of the fittest.

We could hear Dan Singh singing a hundred yards away. Still, perhaps he was better than Hussain who would make himself comfortable on an empty bed while the sweeper, who was only an underling, had to keep guard outside. As soon as he heard our footsteps on the concrete path, he would rush into the ward and a few moments later, a bleary eyed Hussain would come out, vehement in his denials of ever having been asleep. But one night his guard let him down. After shaking the sweeper awake on the verandah we went into the ward and, there on an empty bed, nicely tucked up under the mosquito net and snoring loudly, was Ahmed Hussain. What's more, instead of being apologetic, he was just furious with the sweeper for letting him down!

Sister Shipton was nervous of going about alone, as on one of her past night-duties, the other sister had been attacked by a wandering, drunken American. One of the sweepers went to her rescue and, drawing a little sharpened bamboo stick, he stabbed the man in the throat and killed him. This story I found strangely comforting, as I soon realised that the sepoys had a real respect and affection for their 'Sister Sahibs' – and most of them would have done the same as that sweeper. There had been an Army enquiry but the sweeper was let off, as it was proved that he was defending the Q.A. Sister.

The hospital round over, we would go to the office next to the theatre, which we made our H.Q. for the night. It was central, and also had a pull-plug lavatory next door which was quite a treat to use after our thunderboxes. I made tea and, after discussing the patients, we would settle down to read, or to write letters.

On the British side of the hospital we V.A.D.s were called 'Nurse.' But on the Indian side, the different titles, Q.A.s, Sisters and Nurses were all too complicated. So we were all called 'Sister Sahibs,' but the difference in rank was clearly shown in that the Q.A.s were the 'Burra Sister Sahibs' while we V.A.D.s were the 'Chota Sister Sahibs.' These were the Urdu words for senior and junior.

There were two sweepers for the hospital at night but they liked to go around together as they were nervous of devils, so every now and then there would be a loud cry of 'Sweeper,' which at first I took to be Sister and would leap up. Most nights, we weren't busy and there was just a routine Round each hour. In the morning I would again go to the Surgical ward and help with beds and the washing of ill patients.

We had a good breakfast when we came off-duty, and then to bed in the special night-duty hut. It was still very hot and humid, so I was glad to be up by tea-time to have a bath and dress, and we were allowed to entertain visitors for tea in the Mess. To get into our grounds, a visitor had to write his name and whom he was visiting on a slate, which was nailed to a pole, and then a guard would carry it around until he found the right hostess. Some funny things were written on this board at times. One afternoon, "Dr Jekyl and Mr Hyde for Miss Robertson." announced my doctor friend from the Gurkha party. He took me out to the local Planters club to watch the weekly tennis, then back for early dinner and on duty at 8 p.m.

The Indian doctors were mostly very good but some of them were heartless to their low-caste patients, definitely not taking the same trouble as they would for an officer. Sister explained this to me when one night a bad burns case was admitted to an Indian surgical ward. He was a coolie from the Indian State Labour Units, or IS.LU. as we soon learned to call them. Sister sent for the orderly officer and he arrived grumbling at her for calling him from his bed. She showed him the patient and then, to my surprise, left me to help him while she continued round the hospital.

The man's back was in a fearful mess and his whole condition very shocked. Nothing daunted, the doctor started to clean him up and ripped off great pieces of burnt skin. The patient was in very real pain and I could bear it no longer, and rushed off to Sister. "Please come. He will kill him, I gasped.

She took it quite calmly: "If I go I will only be rude to him, so you must go back and stop him yourself. You'll find that he won't mind."

On my return, I hesitatingly said, "Wouldn't it be better to leave him until he gets over the shock?"

He straightened up with relief.

"Yes Sister, a good idea. Just put on a wet dressing." He left, pleased at having put off a tiresome job for someone else next day. Needless to say, I fetched Sister and together we did what we could for him.

Another time, while on my own, I found a nursing sepoy standing by while a sweeper was trying to help a very ill patient back to bed after using a bedpan on the floor. I motioned the nursing sepoy to help him, but he indignantly refused and went off. Then, in my ignorance, I, myself, helped the sweeper steady the man back into bed. On my return to our office, I found this nursing sepoy putting in an official complaint to Sister that the Chota Sister had told him to do sweeper's work. After dismissing him, she explained to me, "It is absolutely no good, Nurse. Every sister has felt like you do when they first came out, and tried to change things. But it is impossible. What the sepoy should have done was to get the second sweeper to help." She also warned me that, if we helped with the bedpans, we would only lose caste ourselves in the Indians' eyes. "It's no good Nurse, we just can't change things." There was still so much to learn.

After seven nights, Sister Shipton changed for another, who took her duties less seriously. When we started the evening round, she said that, as the hospital was not busy, she had invited in some friends for tea at 9 p.m, so would I please do the medicines on the Indian side, and she would do a thorough round later on. I didn't mind and rather enjoyed giving the medicines out. I dished out the two evil-tasting bottles to all who asked for them, and they rubbed their stomachs appreciatively. I never ceased to marvel at how they could open their throats and the liquid would go down without a swallow. Sister had made it clear that I wasn't welcome while she entertained so, when I had finished, I took refuge in the Surgical ward and drank cups of tea with the orderly. After this, I always made myself scarce when she had any visitors and we got on well. She found it difficult to sleep during the heat of the day so believed in having an hour's snooze during the night. But she was fair, and said I could too, and so in turn we put our feet up and dozed for an hour. During the first hospital round she pointed out any patient for me to watch especially, and then said that we would take the rounds alternately, each on our own. So, altogether the night became easier.

One evening, when making my way back to the British side, I saw a figure in British battledress wandering around. When nearer, I called out asking if he was lost. At that he stumbled and fell flat on the ground. Goodness, was this a drunk that I had been warned about? When I shone my lamp on him. I found that he was an officer in jungle green, and quite exhausted. He had been flown out from 36 Division as a malaria case and somehow got lost at the airfield, and had now only just arrived. I showed him to Officers' ward, and handed him over to the night orderly. Next evening, he apologised if he had frightened me, saying, "I saw your lamp coming, beside a pair of khaki trousers. When I heard a woman's voice, I got such a shock that I tripped and fell over." That must be the only time that anyone had literally fallen flat for me!

The hospital was dimly lit so we each carried a hurricane lamp both to see where we were going and then what to do when we did get to the wards. After 5 p.m. all mosquito nets were put down and well tucked in round the beds, so that the wards looked dim and ghostly sights. The netting was quite thick and one had to peer closely to see the patient inside. "Make sure too, Nurse, that there is only one man in each bed," Sister had warned. I didn't really know what she meant and fortunately never had to discover.

The only nervous moments I had were caused by animals. It had started raining again so the cows decided that it was better to come into the wards or onto the verandahs for shelter. I wasn't frightened of the cows, but the bull, with its big humped back, looked very alarming at first sight. Sometimes he lay down on a path between the wards and only had to snort for me to feel that it was the lesser evil to make a detour and get wet myself. Once I called a sepoy, who laughed and slapped him on the back and made him move away. But I never got on back-slapping terms with that bull. Cows are sacred animals to Hindus and no-one minded their lying down in the wards. Once I woke a nursing sepoy up and, pointing at two cows, told him to send them out. He seemed to think it very fussy of me and I had to tell him twice before he would move. However, the next night that I found him asleep with his head on the table, he came to very quickly. There was another sleeper beside him, but he had come from the Mental ward next door.

One time, I was giving a Morphia injection. In those days there were no prepared ampoules, so we had to boil a tablet in a teaspoon of water held over a little methylated stove. Once, in the semi-dark of the ward office, the light from the flame attracted a bat and, to my horror, it landed on my hand. I didn't scream, but dropped the spoon, and then had to start all over again.

On and off came the weird howling of Jackal packs as they hunted in the Tea-gardens around. As darkness fell, their Banshee-like wails were frightening. Soon we realised that out there they were harmless to us, and then they became just another background noise.

Mary was a sweet white goat who had originally come up as part of the rations, but someone relented and she soon became the pet of the British wards. There was competition for her attention, and patients were even known to hide her down their beds. It was one of my jobs to find her and turn her off her chosen bed, but we all turned a blind eye if she was wise enough to choose an empty one on a verandah. The only complaints I heard about her, was of her drinking tea. She would sneak into a kitchen and drink out of the patients' tea-buckets.

One night, I got a fright while doing the 2 a.m. medicines on an Indian ward. It was important for M and B tablets to be given regularly every four hours. I found that the ward had run out of these tablets and sent the nursing sepoy off with a note to a surgical orderly, asking to borrow some. While he was gone I sat in the office waiting. I noticed the bamboo door opening very, very slowly, one inch, then two inches, then it stopped and no one came in. It was dark outside and I thought someone must be peering in at me. I remembered the Mental ward further along. I could stand it no longer and jumped up and threw the door open. I saw no one but then, on looking down, there on the floor, goggling at me, was a big, fat frog.

Frogs were nice things and were to be encouraged as they ate insects. So too were the lizards that crawled on the walls and they must have accounted for a lot of mosquitoes. These were everywhere, buzzing around. In spite of wearing long sleeves, I had been bitten every night where my shirt touched my skin. It was a hospital joke that if a patient didn't have malaria when he came in, he certainly would have it by the time he left. There were no anti-malaria tablets in those days. Alcohol was the only preventative, as much a psychological booster as anything else. The officer patients were allowed a tot of whisky each night, while the other ranks, both British and Indian, with the doctor's permission, were given rum. Of course, a good Mohammedan always refused his rum, as his religion would not allow him alcohol.

One evening, on reporting to the Surgical ward, the Sister met me. She said, "I have some very sad news, Nurse. Gunner White has died." The whole ward was in gloom and I certainly missed his cheerful "thik hai Nurse" that he had greeted me with each evening.

5

On 15th October, I was glad to come off Night Duty. It was good to be back in the daytime world and to hear what the others had been doing. Mail had come through at last and it was great to have contact with home again, also to have letters from the many friends we had made since our arrival in India. I had the day off and that evening Verity and I went to dinner at the HQ Mess at Dibrugarh to see the Festival of Lights. Dibrugarh was a small town but the capital of Northern Assam and had some Government bungalows and offices and also a little Christian church. It was on the banks of the Brahmaputra, a very wide river, and in the distance, on the other bank, was a line of green jungle. River boats plied up and down carrying both supplies and passengers to lower Assam. The V.A.D.s who were attached to the hospital there, 49 I.G.H., had all travelled up that way instead of by rail. There was a big club which was the centre of entertainment for both civilians and officers. Also a good sized bazaar, or shopping area, though the little we might want to buy was very expensive. That evening, the whole place looked very pretty with every little house and shop lit up with hanging lanterns and lights. Everyone was out in the streets in their best clothes and there was a great air of gaiety. The whole setting was fascinating, but I could hardly keep my eyes open.

No one could help being busy with parties and dates most evenings. The Messes around asked us out and, once a week, there was a cinema and dancing at the local Planters' Club. For all these things, we had to have an escort and could never go out on our own. There were units of Americans around, but we soon developed a feeling of loyalty to our own British troops who thought that Americans were better paid and had so much more in welfare and entertainments. Anyway, Matron had a rule that none of her sisters were to go to an American party without a

British officer as escort to come home with – so we didn't get many American invitations!

However, one afternoon two charming Americans called on our Mess and were invited in for tea by Matron. They had brought an invitation for us all to go to a dance at Ledo. "I am sorry,' said Matron, "I must refuse as that is much too far away."

"That's no trouble, Ma'am. We'll fly the girls," said one of them.

Most of us then looked up with interest, for flying to a dance – that would be exciting. Matron, though, looked horrified. She had a sudden vision of a plane crash and the loss of her entire staff.

"I am sorry, Captain, that would be quite impossible," she said.

There was an amusing evening when a party of us went out with some British officers of an Indian regiment. They knew the country well, and one of them had a pass to go over the river that marked the political boundary of Northern India. We drove for miles, first through tea gardens and then along a jungle track and, after two hours, parked in a clearing miles from anywhere. It was a treat to be away from people and crowds, and there was a wonderful peace, in which could be heard the jungle noise of a buzz of a myriad of insects. The driver lit a camp fire and fixed up lighting and we had a delicious barbecue supper. They produced a gramophone and, afterwards we danced in the moonlight. We felt very daring to be so far into the wild, though the noise of the gramophone must have frightened any wild beasts away for miles around. The daring ones were our hosts, who would have got into a fearful row if their truck had broken down and we had been stuck out there. But we got back safely in the early hours of the morning.

Penny was full of the young man she had met at the brigadier's party and she was going out a lot with Andy. Having safely got our group to Panitola, I no longer felt responsible for them. But Penny was so happy and just couldn't resist telling a new audience about him. I remember trying to pour cold water on her romance. I spoke to her like an old aunt, saying that life was so unnatural that she should think twice about falling for him, and certainly not get married. "I certainly never would out here," said I.

I was now on Officer's ward, having at first a very easy time.

One Sister, myself and two nursing orderlies looked after a dozen not very ill patients, plus, of course the three ward servants. Then news came through that Lord Munster was arriving from England to tour the forward areas to see what conditions were like and what welfare was needed. A few weeks before, a new colonel had taken over and he was the proverbial "new broom". Everything had to be perfect and the whole hospital went into a flat spin. All half days were cancelled and everyone put to scrubbing, polishing and painting. A gang of workmen dug some flower beds in front of the hospital. There was plenty of labour but not many implements, so two men were put on each spade. One man dug it in, and the second pulled it out by a rope attached to the head of the prongs. In, out – in, out – in, out. They worked very quickly, and it was fascinating to watch.

Lady Slim, the G.O.C.s wife, also came round on a tour of inspection and stayed the night in our Mess. She was very charming and normally would have been made a great fuss of – at least we had a good dinner that evening – but we were all too busy spitting and polishing for the V.I.P. to come.

The Colonel decided that the officers must have an ante-room to sit in and gave us furniture which we all helped to paint. British other ranks usually wore white shirts in bed, but on the big day they were all changed into officers' pyjamas and were told, "Don't dare to dirty them before he has been." As a final touch, Officers' ward was issued with two toast racks – not that they ever had any toast to eat.

The big day came and Lord Munster arrived. He looked very unassuming, but was followed by a large entourage of red-tabbed staff. As our ward was near the entrance gate, all inspections started with us, and at least we got them over quickly. He walked right past the smiling young subalterns and stopped at a middle aged captain, with gastric trouble and a sour expression. He asked how things were, and got told the lot. One wireless for the whole hospital, no gramophones, books or magazines, food was hopeless and no decent English cigarettes. He really told the whole story while the staff stood by in silence. When they had gone, Sister, I and the other patients were full of praise to him for his candour and courage.

Lord Munster certainly had an eye for picking the right man. In one of the other wards, he asked a patient, "Do you always wear those pyjamas?" and smiled when he heard the truth. He was certainly a good man for the job and improved things for the 14th Army. The troops felt that at last they were being thought of, and soon plenty of English cigarettes arrived.

It was sometime before any of our officer patients were able to have clean pyjamas, but otherwise we just sank into a state of waiting. I say 'waiting' because everyone knew that the 36 Divison had taken over from the Chindits, and they were getting ready for a big push south into Burma. Most of our patients were from there and they knew that when they returned to their units, they would soon be going into action.

A week later there was an excitement. An ENSA concert was to be given in one of the empty wards. I was on duty until 8 p.m. and so missed the first part, and tried to slip quietly into a seat at the back. However, our up-patients had kept me a seat in the front row and were watching out for me. They signalled and called me, and then one of them came back and joined me. The rest of the audience, or rather the male part of it, thought this a great joke and clapped and whistled, and gave me a much better reception than any of the performers had. "You idiot," I hissed at him, "just look at Matron's face."

I wasn't surprised when, next morning, ward changes were announced and Nurse Robertson was to move to Ward 10. This was the Indian Surgical ward. There were several bad burns cases, including the admission we had had on night duty and who, I was glad to find, was doing well. The staff were Sister, I and some nursing sepoys, plus a sweeper and, of course, two sets of ward boys to deal with the Hindu and the Mohammedan food. None of them spoke English. However, I found it an interesting and rewarding few days. I spent the mornings doing dressings and alternated the afternoon and evening duties with the Sister.

Most of the patients came from very poor homes and lived in what in England would have been thought squalor. They were not used to medical attention and life was very cheap. These men were prepared to put up with more pain and discomfort than would our British troops, and they were all so grateful for what we did for them. However, there were others, mostly of a higher caste who would writhe in their beds in pretended agony, in hopes of getting more attention.

Our surgeon, Major Kelly, was an I.M.S. Regular. The patients had great faith in this English doctor, who both understood and admired them so well. He would scold and shout at them, but they knew that he would always do his best for all of them. One evening he came round, and I asked him to look at a man who kept crying out about his foot. Major Kelly looked at it, solemnly, noting the small cut that was healing nicely. He then turned to me and speaking in a stage whisper, and in Urdu, told me, "If his foot hurts him any more, send him to me and I shall cut it off." From that moment, the man was cured and up and around in no time.

It was after this that he explained to me about the different races of people in India. He pointed to our "groaner" and said that he came from a non-fighting people. "But if you ever hear a Gurkha crying out, then you know he must be dying." Another time, there was a man with a fractured leg who was always asking for his splint to be taken off. The surgeon gave him a real dressing down, ending up with the threat that he would be discharged next morning if he made any more noise. I had a wonderful vision of him being pushed out to the Discharge Parade, bed and all, and found it difficult not to laugh. However, the patient believed it and from then on, made a quick recovery.

I was only on Ward 10 for a few days, as soon as I sprang a temperature and was off with a fever. My last evening on duty, I wrote a quick letter to a nursing friend in England, "I am writing this with the report, but have had a hectic evening up until now, and have a splitting headache. You can't imagine what it is like. The smell is awful. Everyone talks at once, and as loudly as possible, and they all do exactly as they like. In fact, they behave just like children, and it takes an awful lot of patience not to lose my temper. One of the 'haemorrhoids' has just pulled his dressing tube out because it hurts him, and all four of the operation cases are moaning away. There is only one electric light bulb in the ward, and I am going round the beds with a torch. It just seems a mad-house." But this was an evening when I was ill myself. The first few days I had really enjoyed.

That night, Verity reported me sick. It was taken for granted that I must have malaria, and blood slides ordered. Each one came back negative and each time the doctor said, "Bad slide. Take another." In all, eight slides were taken, including one by Matron, and in desperation, the last two by the lab-assistant himself. After two days, I was packed off on a stretcher to the local Mission Hospital. There, I found that I was treated as an interesting case, gently sponged down, put on sulphonamide tablets and not allowed to do anything for myself. Next morning, I woke up feeling much better, but a rash over my face and chest. It was German Measles. What a come down!

St. Luke's Mission Hospital was run by some truly wonderful British women, including a lady doctor who had been given an award for the work that she did receiving refugees from Burma when the Japs moved in. That, however, was only a small part of the work. She had been out there for years looking after the sick of the very poor who could afford no other hospital. A kindly sister looked after me and I think there were some other nurses as well. Theirs was a truly Christian work, and you could see it shining from their faces. They had one ward of private rooms which the army had booked for sick nursing staff.

They treated me, and my German Measles as a good joke, but insisted on my staying in bed owing to the high fever I had had. I would have got very bored if it hadn't been that suddenly an ambulance with half a dozen of my old patients from Officer's ward arrived. Action had started in Burma for the 36 Division, and so the ward was cleared ready for the casualties that would be coming in. Brian Byrnes, who had originally fallen at my feet on night duty, was one of them and also David Carpenter. They were both on lengthy malaria courses to clear it out of their systems, and so were in St. Luke's for even longer than I. When they heard that I was there, they all got permission to visit me, which meant sitting on chairs on the verandah while I sat inside my room.

We had no books, wireless, or newspapers except what Verity and others kindly brought us. So we all just talked and talked. Weeks later, at Panitola, a book arrived for me from David, and in the front he had written, "En mémoire de quelques heures au soleil". It sounded very romantic, but was just when some young men sat in the sun talking to a spotty-faced girl in the shadows inside.

When I was better and up and about, we were allowed to go for walks in the Tea Gardens around the hospital. David and Brian had both been at University when war broke out, and now they both wondered what they would do when peace came. Brian's father had been a professor in Hong Kong, and he and his wife were prisoners of the Japs. Brian and his sister had had just one card from them, and that was all. He worried that they would need his help when they got back and that he must have a job that could keep them too. Then there was the continual worry that they all had – what was happening to the battalion? Every one of them had this guilty feeling that it was wrong for them to be there in safety when they should be facing the same dangers as their men. It was the recurring theme and they would worry and worry as to what was happening.

When at last I got my discharge, Brian was sent as escort in my ambulance. We arrived at the Sisters' Mess and I went in to find hardly a soul about. Not even Home Sister. All were in the hospital and the servants were taking it easy in their absence. I dropped my case in my room and returned to find a forlorn looking Brian standing by the ambulance.

On impulse I said, "Look, no one knows that I'm back. There's a Chinese restaurant in Tinsukia. Let's hitch a lift, and have lunch." So we did, and felt like a couple of naughty school children missing school. It was a delicious lunch too. We got another hitch back, and I was dropped off at the Mess and slipped in un-detected. I changed into slacks and shirt and went in to tea and to report to Matron. She was pleased to see me as they were very busy in the hospital, and told me to go straight on duty and report to the Officers' ward.

Some time later, a box of chocolates arrived for me from Firpos in Calcutta, ordered by Lt. Byrnes. I wrote to him at his unit to thank him. The letter was returned to me by his adjutant who regretted that, 'Lt. Byrnes has been killed in action.' I was so glad that I had suggested that Chinese lunch at Tinsukia: he had only been back a week with his unit when he was killed.

6

There is a blank in my diary until nearly Christmas, nor did I write many letters. So I have no facts to copy from, only some very vivid recollections.

All off-duty had been stopped and we worked from 8 a.m. in the morning until 8 or 9 in the evening, with just an hour for lunch and then the afternoon tea break, for bathing and changing. Day after day after day, we worked harder than I would have thought possible. Every single one of us, sisters, V.A.D.s and orderlies. Nor did we mind as it was nothing to what our patients had been through. In fact, I remember it as both a happy and really fulfilling time. At last, we were of use after all our journeying, good times and hanging about. There was a great feeling of camaraderie; the sisters were only too glad to have our help and, at last, we were accepted as one of US. No-one referred to us as V.A.D.s; we had become "the nurses".

Matron also won much admiration for her common sense way of cutting red tape, and just making the best use of what staff there was. Officially, the Senior Sister was always "Home Sister". She did the housekeeping, was in charge of the servants and generally looked after our health and welfare. Well now, Matron changed this. Home Sister was moved into the hospital where her nursing was needed. Nancy, one of our V.A.D.s with, perhaps, the least nursing experience, but who had a Domestic Science Diploma, was put in as "Home Nurse". However, she only had until 10 a.m. for her housekeeping, and after that she, too, was back in the wards, nursing.

Sister Baptie was now in charge of Officers' ward. She was a tall, strapping young woman, a terrific worker with a great sense of fun. We had had two orderlies on the ward, who really just waited on the officers and did little nursing. Now, they moved to Other Ranks' wards, where their nursing experience could be used. This left Sister and myself to look after about twenty patients who were mostly pretty ill and needed much lifting and looking after. Here again, red tape was cut. Any up-patients who volunteered might stay on and work for us in between their treatment. Some of the malaria and amoebic dysentery cases needed several weeks in hospital. Normally they would be sent back to base, and then, perhaps, on to convalesence. It might be weeks, or months, before they got back to their battalions, nor would they have any news as to what was going on there. Casualties were flown out from 36 Division to two other hospitals as well, but we were the only one with an Officers' ward so, as long as they could hang on with us, they kept contact with their units, and hoped to get back all the sooner.

The Colonel gave his consent, and several of these patients stayed on with us, sleeping out on the verandah. They became invaluable. They helped with everything: bed-making, fetching, carrying, making us cups of tea, and also jellies and milk drinks for the sick patients. When the sweeper was off, they even gave bedpans and bottles – or anyway emptied them for us after we had dealt with very ill patients. They were really better than orderlies as, poor dears, they could never go off-duty. They worked so very hard, partly I think because they felt it was a way of helping their battalions. They would rush at each new casualty that came in to ask what was happening back in their units. They all had this same worry that they should be out there fighting and not sitting in a hospital. Still, the work they did was the best therapy of all, and they would go back to their units with morale high.

These up-patients' only perk was in doling out the evening tot of whisky. As a good many patients were not allowed it, Sister turned a blind eye to what was happening to the rest of the ration. It went out on to the verandah, where, after we had gone, they shared it out among themselves. One man woke in the night yelling that there was a jackal under his bed. Nobody believed him, or gave him any sympathy, as he had had the job of pouring out the whisky that evening.

Ambulance trains arrived twice a week and took all the other patients who weren't on the seriously ill list down to Base

Hospitals. The mornings that they came were hectic, getting the patients ready and onto stretchers and off. Then there were their beds to remake ready for fresh casualties that might arrive in the afternoon. Of course, there were still our "dangerously" and "seriously ill" patients to be looked after, and nothing could be neglected.

Many a man owed his life to the skill of our surgeons. After that, the general atmosphere of cheerful work and laughter helped them to recover, and ours was a happy, homely ward.

On a routine morning, when we came on duty, Sister would do a quick round of the ward, then settle down to the books and get the work planned for the day. In the meantime, I got the dressing room ready, boiled up the instruments, filled up the dressing drums and sent them off to be sterilized, and generally saw that the ward servants were doing their work. Then we would do the beds together all round the ward. I had learned in England the knack of lifting patients. So long as I did it with someone else also trained that way, I had no trouble in lifting the heaviest of men. It was later in the day, lifting patients with only up-patients to help, that I found it exhausting. They lifted by sheer brute strength, and I would find my side very heavy indeed.

I think that I must have been back at work for about ten days when I exploded with rage at the pani-wallah. It was at the end of the day, and Sister had gone off to give in her report to the night staff and had left me to finish off. I went into the kitchen and found the ward-boy with a big pile of dirty dishes still to wash up, while the pani-wallah leant against the wall watching him. I told him to help with the washing up and he replied that it wasn't his work. My Urdu wouldn't suffice, so I really let fly in English. He couldn't understand what I was saying but did realise how very angry I was.

All my tiredness and pent up emotion burst out. I shouted that he was, "a lazy, good for nothing," who never did a hand's turn for anyone, and so on and so on. I didn't actually swear, for we didn't really know how to in those days. He gazed at me, horrified, for all he knew I was calling down curses on him and his children's children. I walked out of the kitchen only to find that the whole ward had heard every word through the thin bamboo walls. There was a silence with no one saying anything. Nor did I, or I might have burst into tears.

Next morning, out of sheer fright, the pani-wallah went off sick, and the man who replaced him became a great success. He was from the Punjab, and knew even less Urdu than I. Always smiling and helpful, never minding what he did, he soon got the nickname 'Gunga Din'. I never had any trouble with ward servants again, and must have earned quite a reputation.

Someone must have said something to Sister, as she brought the subject of tiredness up. When I admitted it, she said, "I'm tired too, but I couldn't say so when you are so much smaller than me. From now on, we must each try to get two hours off-duty each day, or we'll never be able to keep up this pace."

This sensible rest did wonders and we really got through more work in the end. However rushed we were, every patient got his treatment. The only time that we would actually sit down was at about 12.45 p.m. After first lunch in the Mess, the mail was given out and whichever of us went first, collected the letters for both of us, and we would sit in the office and read them with a cup of tea. This time was sacrosanct and no one disturbed us unnecessarily. Sister Baptie was engaged to an officer whom she had met at Imphal, and he wrote to her every day. Sometimes, they were delayed and arrived in batches, but he never missed writing, and his letters meant so much to her. So, we would sit and read our letters and she would discuss the patients with me, and it was a peaceful time of day.

There were four British battalions in the 36 Division under the command of General Stilwell, and they and his Chinese troops were fighting their way down the railway from Myitkyina, to join up later with troops coming in from Imphal. I was able to tell Verity that her Peter's lot were not yet in action, which helped as this was a very worrying time for her.

She and Peter wrote regularly but letters took days to travel between us and Kohima where he was stationed. Perhaps it was as well that we were so busy and she didn't have much time to think and worry. He had written that he hoped to get another leave, and she had promised to marry him then, but nothing could be planned ahead. However, she never bothered us with all this. She was the perfect roommate, tolerant, kind and always cheerful and full of a quiet courage which later was to stand her in good stead. I, myself, never worried about Peter. Their meeting in Calcutta was so extraordinary that I felt sure that it was meant, and that he would be back again to marry her. Perhaps Verity felt the same herself.

One afternoon, we had a big batch of casualties. One of the battalions had had a bad time with four officers killed and four more came in to us wounded, as well as some from other regiments. A surgeon came in to make out a list for immediate operations, and I started getting the new patients ready for his inspection. There was a captain with a bad stomach wound, over which the First Aid Station had put a wad of dressing covered with wide strips of Elastoplast. Using surgical spirit, I was trying to get this off as gently as possible, when I heard a voice behind me. "Come on, Nurse. Rip it off. I've no time to pamper officers." I whipped round, surprised at the curt voice, and then saw Major Kelly's tired face. He had been operating for hours on end, and now would be going on most of the night. So, I pulled the plaster off firmly, but as gently as possible. The patient went deathly white, but made no sound. The surgeon turned to Sister, "Right, this one first, and then him," pointing at a second abdominal case.

There were two surgeons, but only one theatre sister. Though she had a good staff of trained orderlies, she still had the main responsibility. That evening we gave her two eggs from our ward which she could whip up with some milk to get a little extra energy when she needed it.

Another casualty brought in that day was a major, badly shot in the legs. He had been rescued from open ground by one of his subalterns, who had crawled out and dragged him back to safety. This young man followed next day with a wounded arm. As soon as he arrived, he asked after his major, and was so thankful to find him still alive. This subaltern was awarded an Immediate M.C.

At first it was mainly gunshot wounds that came in. Then there was a pause while our troops were held up over marshy ground. This was a clever trick of the Japs as they knew that the area was infected with Bush Typhus – or Tick Typhus. Soon patients poured into the hospital with that dread disease, for which there was no known medical cure. Only rest, and lots of good nursing helped a little but the trouble was that we just didn't have enough nurses.

The two "stomachs", as they were soon called, were in beds next to each other on one side of the ward. They were on a very strict, and small fluid diet and, as they got better they soon got hungry. Opposite them was our first Typhus case. As he was the first, for the sake of morale, it was kept secret and his temperature chart marked 'Malaria'. This was alright until the Stomachs started getting hungry, then it became torture to them to watch me coaxing the boy to eat. They snarled, "Why do you fuss over him so much? He only has malaria." They looked like a couple of very hungry, greedy dogs, and we saw how awful it was for them to have to see him actually refusing food. So the secret had to come out, though by this time his first crucial days were over, and he was on the mend. He made a wonderful recovery, and was a great example to later cases that came in. "See how well 'Typhus' is? If you eat up you'll soon feel as good as him."

Sadly though, we did have one officer die of Typhus. The only death that we had on that ward, for any cause.

The Medical wards were full of it. Typhus cases came flooding in and the Medical side could hardly cope. But there was a wonderful spirit in the hospital, and everyone rose to the challenge and helped out as best they could. For a few days we, on Officers', had a small Typhus ward of about twenty attached to us – some distance away with a Surgical ward in between, and somehow we managed. Major Grundstein, the Medical Specialist, made his headquarters there at a desk by the door. When he could he worked with us, helping with the illest patients, and keeping at it as hard as anyone.

I remember well one day leaving him in charge of the ward while I went over to Officers' to do some treatments. When I came back what did I see but our Medical Specialist sitting immersed in his papers. "Major Grundstein," I said in horror. At the tone of my voice he turned, and when he saw where I was looking he certainly jumped. For there, sitting on the dirty dressing bucket which he was using as a bedpan, and grinning at us, was one of our dangerously ill Typhus patients. Together we cleaned him up and got him back to bed.

The patients arrived exhausted after their journey, and many wanted nothing but to be left alone to die quietly. It was tragic to see. They were so apathetic, except for the really bad cases who became delirious, and for whom there was little hope. They all needed bed-baths, and then much attention to strengthen them with nourishing drinks and light food. Our officer up-patients helped too, and I remember a major who went round taking temperatures. The patients were too ill to wonder why the men looking after them wore pyjamas.

Officers' ward soon collected its own quota of typhus cases, so our extra ward had to be passed back to the Medical side. However, we had helped out over the first rush, and now we too were hectic, with battle casualties coming in as well.

Verity was on an Indian Medical ward that was frantically busy too. She found it difficult to get used to the M.O.s fatalistic outlook. He would stop her attending to some of the really ill patients. "He will die, Sister. He will die. We can do nothing." At first it worried her, but at least she had more time for the other patients. On looking back I can see that as the doctor was a good Hindu, he would believe that the patients would be going on to a new and probably better life. So why should we try to drag him back to this? Still, there was no time to philosophise just then.

We had no Hospital Chaplain, nor one that ever visited us. Probably this was because we were a combined hospital. If we had a Christian clergyman, then we should also have had priests for the Hindus, Mohammedans, Buddhists and perhaps other sects as well. The mind fairly boggles at the religious squabbles and fusses that would have come up.

However, things got better. Help was sent by G.H.Q. in the form of a special Typhus Unit of Q.A. Sisters who were flown in to the Casualty Clearing Station, behind the fighting lines, to set up a temporary ward there for Typhus patients. For it was during the first few days that the patients needed complete rest. Now with this special nursing they soon became strong enough to make the long journey back to us. First on an ambulance train pulled by a jeep (as the Japs had left no serviceable engines) along the railway line that our troops had fought for and recovered. Then by air to

Dinjan Airfield, followed by a bumpy ambulance drive to our hospital. So soon the Typhus cases reached us in a better state, and before long could be passed on to Base Hospitals.

During the first rush of them, one very busy evening in Reception, a man was brought in who was thought to be dead. The ambulance sepoys were new to the job and didn't know where to put him among the confusion of stretchers around. So, without ceremony they dumped him straight into the Mortuary. Fortunately for him, later that evening another man died and was taken down to join him. What should the wretched Indian stretcher bearers find, but a corpse that sat up and looked at them.

Gibbering with fright, they dashed back yelling that there was a devil in the Mortuary. Night-sister grabbed an orderly and together they raced down, and indeed they found that the man was still alive. They got him back to Reception, where she worked on him most of the night, and very definitely saved his life. Night-sister tried to keep the story secret – deadly secret – but next morning when he was moved into a ward, one of the other patients recognised him.

"That's Corporal . . . ," he said. "He was dead last night. I know he was, because I was in the ambulance with him."

Perhaps his trip to the Mortuary actually saved his life. For he naturally became a very special patient, and had every nursing care which couldn't always be spared for the others.

After a few weeks he was well on the way to recovery, and was evacuated back to a hospital in India. He had a story to tell which may have earned him free beers for many a year!

During this hectic time, a patient who was being evacuated by ambulance train, called me over. "I've a present for you, Nurse," and he unpacked his haversack and handed me a bundle to unwrap. Inside some old clothes I found a gilded figure of a sitting Buddha.

"Please have it," he said pleadingly. "I haven't really the space to take it back to India."

"How on earth did you get that?" I asked astounded.

"It was in a ruined temple. If I hadn't taken it, an American would," he added defensively.

So I took it back to my room and solemnly stood it on the chest of drawers. The surprise was all too much for Verity, and she burst into laughter. "Now I know the title of a book you could write: "Marian and her Burmese Buddha," and she collapsed into giggles again.

For I had once suggested to the others that our story should be written up. "What would be the good of that?" someone answered. "No one in England would believe us."

For a few days this Buddha sat in our room looking most incongruous, but I soon started feeling horribly uncomfortable when I looked at it. I remembered the oft-told story of my grandmother. She had been given a figure taken originally from an Hindu temple, and depicting Ganesh, the Elephant God. At the same time she was warned that it brought bad luck to whoever had it. "What nonsense," my grandmother said, for she was a strong and single minded Christian who didn't believe in what she called Heathen Gods. So she accepted it as an antique that she would take back to England when they eventually retired, and she would put it up as an ornament in her house.

Within a month she became ill with Cholera, and in thirty six hours she had died. Perhaps a coincidence, but my grandfather didn't think so. He arranged for the figure to be taken to a Hindu temple, and paid money for the correct rituals to be observed.

I felt more and more that this Buddha might bring us bad luck, and anyway it shouldn't be sitting there on show. I didn't know what to do with it as our colonel was an Indian and perhaps would be offended and make trouble for the officer who had given it to me. Everyone was too busy to be bothered with such a thing but I simply must be rid of it. On impulse I asked our bearer if he would like it. He was delighted and his face lit up with real joy. I don't know what religion he was. Perhaps he was a Buddhist, as we weren't far from the Burma border. But anyway, as an Hindu he would respect it. Maybe he sold the little Buddha, but I like to think that he gave it to a priest and so gained merit for a future life.

I was relieved to pass it on for, unlike my grandmother, I had already learnt to respect other religions and realise that there is more than one path to heaven – isn't it just an accident of birth as to where one is born and so which religion one grows up with? This bearer proved a good and honest servant to us, and he stayed with me until I finally left northern Assam.

It was well known that all forward hospitals were badly understaffed so Lady Louis Mountbatten, representing the Red Cross, came round on tour to see things for herself. She flew up to visit the three hospitals in our area, and stayed a night at a planter's bungalow nearby, and we were the first hospital she came to. She was used to inspecting Red Cross Nurses in England, in rows, wearing beautifully clean white aprons, and starched caps pulled well down on the forehead to hide all hair. Well, I had put on a clean dress, but it already looked woefully crumpled. There was a limp string of a cap, pinned on behind my curls, and we didn't wear aprons. She came in followed by Matron and a huge retinue of officers. Matron presented Sister and myself, and Lady Louis turned to her and said, "Dame Beryl Oliver asked me to look out for any V.A.D.s. Do you have any?"

"Yes," Matron said, "Nurse Robertson is a V.A.D."

The tall and beautifully immaculate figure looked down at me, and was taken aback at what she saw. "She's rather a small one," said Lady Louis.

There was a moment of embarrassed silence as I stood speechless. Then Sister, bless, her, said, "Yes, but she's a very efficient one," quickly adding, "and now, let me present to you the hero of our ward." She pushed forward the young subaltern who had just won the M.C. and who looked almost as indignant as me. However, Lady Louis was most interested and gave him her sincere congratulations on being told his tale. Later she and her staff had lunch in our Mess. There were so many high-ranking officers that I found myself seated next to the A.D.M.S. – a senior Medical Officer who usually did hospital inspections himself. But we had a very good lunch indeed, and we heard later that her whole tour did much to help the troops' morale.

Things had already improved since Lord Munster's visit. English cigarettes for the troops and better rations. One effort was a duck farm started by the army near Dibrugarh. A big day came when Officers' ward were allocated some ducks and our patients were looking forward to having them for lunch. I am told that if a bird is cooked immediately after killing, it is nice and tender, which is how the following incident could happen. The main kitchen was behind the wards, and when the cook started to kill the ducks, one escaped. It tore down the ward, quacking and flapping, and out at the front, with the cook racing behind him, brandishing his long kitchen knife. The duck leapt into the 12 foot square water tank outside and floated in triumph in the middle, where neither the cook, nor anyone else, could reach him. There was great excitement in the ward with "Tally-hos," and cheers when the duck got to safety in the water, and where it stayed floating in the middle. But when the patients heard that this was to be part of their lunch, and now there wouldn't be enough, their mood changed. This was serious, and greed took over. An up-patient jumped in and, after stalking, caught the bird and had a double helping at lunch.

The new drug, penicillin, had been issued to the hospital. In those days it had to be injected into the patient regularly every three hours and, in between, the precious liquid kept in a refrigerator. Well, there was only one fridge in the whole hospital, and it was a new and very special drug. So a ward was set up especially for penicillin patients where they could get specialist treatment and injections from Sisters. When any of our patients were put on penicillin, they were moved out to that ward, until the end of their treatment. They were always delighted to get back, not just to their old ward, but to get away from that awful three hourly injection in their behinds.

So often patients were worried as to what they might have said when under an anaesthetic. Many times I was asked, "Did I say anything awful, Nurse?" Of course, very rarely does anyone say anything intelligible, but just occasionally it happened. There was one quite amusing time when a young man came round from an operation on his foot. He was chattering away while being wheeled back into the ward. The patients listened in sympathetic silence, because it was obvious that he thought himself back fighting the war in the jungle.

A patient was sitting by him to watch but once, on passing, I stopped at the end of his bed to see how he was getting on, and he sat up and pointed a finger at me. "If you go outside the perimeter at night," he said accusingly, "then it's your own bloody fault," and sank back again. The ward, of coure, collapsed into guffaws of laughter, and he wasn't allowed to forget what he told me.

During the second week of December, we heard that a Principal Matron was coming round on tour. Not just any P.M., but one out from England to see what conditions were like in the forward hospitals and, as usual, she would come to us first. On the afternoon of her arrival, Sister Baptie said she was going off-duty. I was horrified. "You can't," I said.

"I can. She has come out to see what conditions are like, so she can jolly well see what they are like. Just let this woman see what we have to put up with. Now you stick to the patients' treatment, and don't do any clearing up," and she stamped off full off fire and righteousness. She was what the troops call 'browned off.' She didn't care what happened to herself but, for the sake of the hospital, was out for a good old row.

I rather admired her attitude, but didn't much like the idea of being the first to collect any wrath that would come down. However the up-patients were as startled as me for, as they said, it was like a General's inspection and they insisted on turning to and getting the place tidied and cleaned up. I was busy that afternoon with a delirious Typhus case and didn't have a chance to see what a good job they were making behind the scenes. They got the servants going, cleaning and sweeping and, themselves turned out the medicine cupboard. Then one of them brought me the key and I put it in my pocket. Usually the cupboard was unlocked as there just wasn't time for niceties like that, and anyway most of the up-patients were honorary orderlies and used to fetching medicine for us.

When the Principal Matron arrived at our hospital, her first shock was to find a V.A.D. acting as Home Sister. Then she came on to us. I was actually behind the screens with my Typhus patient, so there were no staff in sight at all. I popped my head out and said that Sister was off-duty. This second shock was even worse. What! A V.A.D. in charge of Officer's ward. Whatever next?

"No Sister on duty? What do you mean," she asked astounded.

"Well, Matron, I can't inspect a ward where the Sister-in-charge is off-duty. I shall come back again to-morrow morning. "But," she added with a sudden gleam in her eye, "The offices are Nurse's reponsibility. I shall inspect them now."

An up-patient had taken over from me behind the screens and I followed the two Matrons, wondering what would happen next. First into the dressings' room – everything clean and tidy. Then the little ward kitchen, where the three Indian staff stood smartly to attention. Next the Sister's office where again everything was spotless. It was all too good to be true. Her eye landed on the medicince cupboard: "Nurse, I should like to see in there please."

I took the key out of my pocket, opened the cupboard doors wide and showed neat rows of beautifully clean bottles. I don't know who was the most surprised, Principal Matron, Matron, or I. As a last resort, Principal Matron said, "Nurse, is that medicine cupboard usually locked, and where is the key kept?"

At her brisk sounding voice I stood to Attention, but then I looked her straight in the face: "Yes, it is locked and the key kept either in Sister's or my pockets." I felt my patients deserved that lie for all their foresight and hard work!

"This all seems satisfactory Nurse, but I shall be back again to-morrow to inspect the ward." And the two Matrons swept out and on round the hospital.

The patients were absolutely delighted with the success of their stratagem, and by now were almost rolling about with laughter. Needless to say I thanked them, but when Baptie arrived back having heard of a story of an open medicine cupboard, she seemed disappointed when she heard it wasn't ours, nor was she at all pleased at the success of the cleaning up, for her blood was still boiling for a good old row.

However, that evening she must have received a real rocket, for it was a different thing next morning, and she was distinctly tight-lipped on the whole affair. We all rushed round getting the ward perfect – beds in straight lines, the lot. When the inspection started, there we were waiting standing to attention by the beds, with everything very official and correct. Yet Sister's courage must have helped to make the big difference that came to our hospital. Signals went out. All future casualties were diverted to other hospitals. At the same time extra sisters started arriving from Base hospitals, including a second theatre sister, so by Christmas we were having a very easy time, whereas the next hospital was working flat out.

Our favourite visitor was the Marchioness of Reading, who came round on tour representing the W.V.S. and stayed the night of New Year's Eve in our Mess. The 14th called themselves 'The Forgotten Army,' and by now we girls almost felt the same way ourselves. But Lady Reading had such a wonderful warm personality and reminded us of all the middleaged Mothers back home. After lunch she sat on in the Mess talking to Dorothy and myself all afternoon, when she must have been longing to put her feet up in her own room. She cheered us enormously, bringing in a breath of fresh air from the world outside.

7

During this time of hard work Verity and I usually collapsed when off-duty straight into beds that had their bottom ends propped up on chairs, to help the aching feet we soon got from a combination of concrete floors and the heat by day.

Penny however, was of tougher fibre than us, or perhaps it was LOVE. While I had German Measles, she and Andy visited me and said that they were engaged. His brigadier was delighted and encouraged an early marriage so that he could give the wedding from his Mess. Penny was in Seventh Heaven and the wedding took place, I think, some time after Christmas with the brigadier giving the bride away. We had a good party and she went off on marriage leave.

Dianne to, had a very busy off-duty time. None of us could quite understand her love-life. Somewhere along the line she had a week's leave and got married in Calcutta. However her social life went on as ever. We muttered darkly amongst ourselves, "It must be because she is half French." Yes, we agreed, that explained everything.

The rest of us generally felt too exhausted when we came off-duty to think about going out, and we were thankful when the extra Sisters arrived after the Principal Matron's signals.

Then what was truly wonderful was that on the evening of Friday 15th December, Peter drove up in a jeep – quite out of the blue. "My colonel has given me orders to fetch Verity back and marry her next Tuesday at Kohima," he announced to me. "He has always refused permission for us to be engaged, but at last he got so fed up with me that yesterday he told me to take a jeep, fetch my girl, and he would have the wedding all laid on for Tuesday. So here I am."

Verity's letters to him must have been mostly free of complaint for he seemed to have no idea at all of the hard work and

65

strain that the hospital had been under. Where he was the big push hadn't yet started, and so the Kohima hospital wasn't too busy. He just took it for granted that Verity would come straight off with him. To top it all he even asked me to go with them too as a Bridesmaid! "No, I'm sorry but I can't," I said feeling quite staggered. "Verity can always apply for marriage leave, but Matron would hit the roof if I asked to go too as her Bridesmaid."

What a thrill it all was, and imagine the excitement among us all! But next morning Matron took a rather different view of things. Here was the same young man with his high-handed ways, expecting to whisk off one of her nurses when none of the Sisters had had leave for months. He might be under his colonel's orders, but she certainly wasn't. So it was only natural that she was sticky and refused their request.

In desperation, Peter went to our colonel with his story. Fortunately the C.O. took a more objective view and also thought the whole thing very romantic. So he overruled Matron, or rather went and persuaded her to give her permission, as luckily it was after the P.M.s visit and the extra Sisters were already arriving. So after all, Verity got two weeks' leave starting from the next day, and this gave her the rest of the day to madly wash, iron, and get packed for the week's honeymoon in Darjeeling.

In the middle of it all Miss Corsar arrived from Delhi. In my letter home I said, "It was nice to see her. She is doing an amazing tour – only Corsar could stand the strain. Travelling continuously and stopping only one night at each place. She says that she has had very good reports about V.A.D.s from every unit, and they are asking for hundreds more of them back in England."

I gave a coffee party for her in my room with Miss Corsar in a chair of honour, and the rest of us spread around on the floor, while Verity washed her hair in the background. Yes, she was wearing the famous Government issue boots held up firmly by her suspenders. By now the evenings had become quite cool, so she wasn't hot in them. Also she wore an air of dignity in her skirt which she mightn't have had in a pair of slacks. Of course, no one but us knew how high her boots went, nor how they were kept up.

Next morning I took a couple of bottles of Gin over to the ward, and Sister Baptie and I gave a little send-off party in the office for Verity and Peter. The up-patients joined us, but two of them slipped out to the jeep which they decorated with white bows and streamers made from bandages. As the happy couple left, they walked through the ward to the cheers of the bed-patients. The rest of us ran outside and gave them a great send-off. With a grinning little Gurkha at the wheel, they departed with all bandages flying, and two old boots – especially issued by Q.M. stores – tied on behind.

Miss Corsar couldn't come to the party as she was closeted in Matron's office getting reports on us ten. In Aldershot a party like ours would have been unthinkable. Especially in the very early days of the War when the Red Cross decreed that V.A.D.s should neither smoke nor drink in public. Of course the result was that most of us took to drinking Gin and Lime – large innocuous looking Lime drinks quietly laced with a little Gin – but now times had changed. Assam was in a different world, and our Commandant would have enjoyed the party.

In the afternoon she interviewed us all separately, and patiently listened to our queries and complaints. Time was so short we didn't hear much of her news. It was many years later that she told me tales of the incredible tour she had made. Unescorted and intrepid, she travelled from hospital to hospital, by air, by riverboat and by train. It was a journey that many male staff officers would have balked at, but she was up-held by a strong sense of duty to the Red Cross and a real feeling of responsibility for the V.A.D.s in her care.

That evening Dorothy and I saw her off on the Night Mail and were really sorry at her going. Her coming had cheered us all up and we none of us felt so cut off and far away.

Harry, afterwards, took us out to dinner at some civilian friends of his, called Findlayson. They had a bungalow near Tinsukia, and were a kindly couple who frequently had tennis and swimming parties for the officers around. Bungalows in Assam were raised quite high off the ground by stilts, perhaps because of flooding, but this also helped to keep mosquitoes away. However, once inside, it seemed the height of luxury.

The army had very sensibly attached ex-planters either to the Pioneer corps or to IS.LU. because of their knowledge of the languages and, more important, the experience they had had in working Indian labour forces on their estates. Harry had been a tea-planter and, though now a Gurkha officer, he was in charge of one of the IS.LU. nearby and, because of Dorothy, we saw a lot of him at our Mess. Mrs Findlayson had introduced them at the Club, and was rather pleased with herself that the romance was going so well. I went there for a few times with Dorothy but, for me, the treat was a real bath with taps that ran hot and cold, and a smiling ayah holding out a big clean bath towel.

Casualties had been diverted to other hospitals and life had already become much easier. The extra Sisters had arrived and the only admittances we had were from local units and, on the Indian side mostly coolies from IS.LU. The Colonel agreed to keep our up-patients in for Christmas and they got busy decorating the ward. "The wards are beginning to look lovely," I wrote home. "The patients have been making paper chains from coloured paper, and painting posters and things, and all getting very excited about it. I've got them a Christmas tree, and the Red Cross are sending parcels for each man, so we shall be able to fill their stockings – and, somehow, the patients have acquired some mistletoe. I think it is going to be a really lovely Christmas, as they are all so thrilled and excited."

Our Medical Officers, though, weren't so happy. One evening, their Mess hut caught fire. It was frightening how high the flames were, and how quickly it burnt. Luckily there was no wind, or sparks might have blown across to the hospital. Major Grundstein, who was what in those days I would have called middle-aged, very bravely climbed up on the roof and tried to douse the flames with a chain of buckets of water passed up to him, but without success. In fact, we heard that he was only criticised by the others for not having seen to the essentials, i.e. saving the hoard of liquor that they had collected for Christmas, and which had now gone up in flames.

There is a great atmosphere in hospital at Christmas, with everyone trying to make it a happy time for the patients. On Christmas Eve, we had a party on our ward including Matron and all the nursing staff, and we danced to a gramophone. Then the M.O.s, sisters and ourselves went round the hospital singing carols. Christmas Day went well. We had a tree with presents on it, and the patients had had stockings. Sister and I were very touched by the ward having gone to great trouble to get us really nice presents. In the evening there was a dance in one of the British wards and I went over there with our up-patients who were to act as M.C.s, having had strict instructions from Sister not to dance themselves. It all went well and the dancing was fun. Then we returned and played paper games on the ward. All so simple, but I think everyone enjoyed themselves very much. On the 27th, the club had a party and Sister Baptie and I took to it our up-patients all dressed up in their uniforms – as I think they had been for all the Christmas parties. On New Year's Eve, we gave them a party in my room, all sitting around the floor. However, like Cinderella they had to be back by mid-night, and we had to see them safely to bed.

Our ward had become quite a close unit, but now had to break up. The up-patients went either to convalescent homes or back to their units, while the bed-patients were gradually moved out by ambulance trains to Base Hospitals. Some of them had been with us for two months or more, and were really sorry to go. The major with the wounded legs and one of the "stomachs" were still both on the dangerously ill list, and so couldn't travel by train. Finally, the Americans offered to fly them down to Calcutta as a gesture of goodwill. One of our Sisters went with them, and said that it was a great publicity stunt, with a photographer from 'Life' magazine taking photos of them. Soon we had letters from both of them, moaning about the strict British Hospital they had been moved to, and urging me to visit when I went on leave to Calcutta.

In the meantime, Verity returned from her honeymoon. When Peter dropped her back at our Mess she had to go straight on duty, at 5 p.m. on her old ward. Feeling absolutely bereft at the parting, and the thought of him going back into action with the battalion, she couldn't face the ward and went into the office and sat there numb with despair.

Then her old nursing sepoy came in with a tray, saying,

"Memsahib, I have made you some tea." The understanding he showed by using her new married title and the kind thought of the tea were too much for her. When he had gone out, she dissolved into tears all over the desk.

She had time to recover and by dinner, she was able to greet us cheerfully, and show the brave face that British people expected. But the warmer hearted Indian sepoys would have thought it only right that she should weep when her husband went off to war. They would have admired and respected her all the more for the tears she shed.

Afterwards, she enthralled us with the tale of her wedding. At Kohima, a place that earlier in the year had been the scene of one of the most bitter and bloody battles of the Burma war, there was this happy wedding with a reception laid on by Peter's Mess.

On their arrival back at his unit Peter found that, though the Bishop had issued a Special Licence for the wedding, the District Commissioner insisted that by law they must wait another five days while he put up their Banns. This entailed a printed notice being nailed up outside his office door for any passing Naga tribesman to read. It sounded very efficient, but was written in long hand by the office clerk and made amusing reading.

According to it, Peter was a 'Mayor' who had lived in Kohima for six months, whereas Verity was a spinster from Panitola, a village in the Naga Hills. The wedding Chapel was the 35th Milestone on the Imphal road.

Having dispatched Peter to fetch his Bride, the young C.O. of 28 years of age – who later rose to being a general – now directed his energies to arranging the wedding. It wouldn't be St Margaret's, Westminster, but he would make sure that it would be a really memorable occasion, not only for the officers but for the whole battalion. He sent one officer off to beg, borrow or buy a harmonium for the service. Another to Base to collect two forty gallon drums of Rum for the men, plus, of course, plenty of alcohol for the Mess. Others were detailed to blast the river with grenades to get fish, still more men to go hunting to shoot Deer and other Game for the feast. Others were told to pitch a large tent to be used as the Church.

So by the time Verity and Peter arrived, there was an aura of tremendous excitement. Luckily the Matron of Kohima hospital was Miss Walden, and she couldn't have been kinder or made Verity more welcome as a visitor to their Mess.

The V.A.D.s all rallied round lending her clothes. One of them produced a long white evening dress for her to be married in. Another a flimsy white scarf for a veil or head-dress, and the whole effect was a very pretty wedding outfit. Verity made a really lovely Bride. Peter had only a specially laundered Bush shirt and trousers.

One of the company commanders was to be Best Man, as he was the old man of the Mess, being at least thirty years old. He took his duties very seriously and, on the Wedding Eve, he saw that Peter stayed reasonably sober and packed him off early to bed – but the others caroused through the night.

The whole of the Kohima Sisters' Mess were invited to the wedding, and for the grand party afterwards. The ceremony was held in a specially erected tent, on Milestone thirty five on the Imphal Road. Peter and Verity walked out afterwards under an archway of Gurkha kukris, and to the cheers of the whole battalion.

The 14th Army line of Communications ran up this road but was completely disrupted, when they finally drove away in a mule-cart surrounded by dancing and cheering Gurkha soldiers. All traffic was stopped for about a quarter of an hour until, a mile further on, they changed into the jeep that was to take them on as far as the rail-head.

They stopped the first night at a Rest-house. Here the Gurkha driver took their luggage in and wrestled with the problem of their bed-rolls, and they watched as he unrolled one on each bed. Then he shrugged his shoulders, put one on top of the other, grinned, and went out!

They had been lent a bungalow at Darjeeling for their honeymoon, where they spent a glorious week before driving back up to Panitola again. Now Verity wouldn't know when she would hear from Peter again. He had given her the address of his H.Q. at Dharamsala, and she knew that if he were killed, or wounded, she would hear from them. The Regiment there would always be responsible for her, but now she had to expect some lonely months ahead. She had one letter from him saying that on his return, he had found the camp-site deserted. The jungle already closing in, and hardly a sign that his troops had been there. They had moved out the day after the wedding, and Peter chased off after them into Burma – and then his letters just stopped coming.

Sometime around then, I had a letter from the Red Cross saying that I had been recommended to go on a special condensed, one year training course to take the examination for an S.R.N. – or State Registered Nurse. Good old Matron Davis back in England. All my years of slogging at the Cambridge hadn't been considered in vain. If only this offer had come a year earlier, but now I felt almost indignant. Back in England they might think that the War was ending, but out here it still looked a long way to finishing. Now, too, I was really needed and replacing a trained Nurse. So without thinking twice, and perhaps foolishly, I wrote straight back, refusing. I don't think I even sounded grateful. It must have been a bit of an honour, as none of the others had that offer.

So I just waited and helped pack off our patients, and wondered how many would get safely through the war and how many would return to their units, only to be killed in action. Poor Verity, how she must have worried about Peter, and I was glad to have the time to keep her company.

8

At New Year, Matron said that we must all put in for the month's Leave that we were due each year. Penny was already away on her honeymoon, and Marian went off to join her doctor husband. I had a cousin Vera, who with her husband Bobs Irwin, lived in Calcutta. Also her brother was stationed at Dehra Dunn, and they both invited me to stay. So I arranged to have my Leave in February before the Hot Weather started. Dorothy's Harry had connections in the American Air Force, and he managed to book me a flight down to Calcutta – all so easy compared to our journey up.

At last February came and Harry saw me off at the airport. Dinjan was busy as it was one of the refuelling posts for transport planes flying 'over the Hump' to Chungking. The Americans had been hard at it building the road from Ledo into China, and I was told that the first convoy had driven through, led by the American General who had been in charge of its making.

The Americans had good welfare arrangements for their troops and laid on passenger planes to fly them to Calcutta, and I had a seat on one of these. I had only flown once before, and then in a little tiger moth plane, so when we finally embarked it all seemed so very spacious and comfortable with its passenger seats. It was exciting lifting off and, when we were airborne, I got a message from the pilot asking me to come forward to sit in the cockpit and so get a better view. What a thrill it was sitting in the co-pilot's seat! It was also fascinating looking down at the panorama of the way we had so slowly chugged up by train, but when word came through that it was to be a bumpy passage and all seat belts were to be fastened, I went back and didn't see who else was travelling with us.

It was dark by the time we arrived at Dum Dum Airport. I went to look for the American bus that I had been told would take us the ten miles into Calcutta. All I could see was what looked like a rather shabby looking G.I. standing waiting on his own. He looked like a bus driver, so I went and asked him if he was going to Calcutta. He said, "Yes," and certainly he would take me.

Just then a smart American officer dashed up, saluted and said, "All ready now, General." General! I was astounded and looked again. He was wearing ordinary jungle green battledress with the small insignia of rank worn when on active service to stop being spotted by snipers, and he was, indeed, a General. In fact, it was General Pick who had built the Ledo Road and led the first convoy into China.

I had a very comfortable journey into Calcutta sitting in the back of the staff car with this very kindly and unostentatious general. He gave orders to drop me at an American transport centre, where his A.D.C. took me and my luggage in with instructions that I was to be given a lift on. The A.D.C. couldn't quite understand what I was doing with the General, so obviously thought that I had better be given V.I.P. treatment, until a message arrived for him to "Come back quick." However, another officer came forward and said that he would drive me on and it was lucky that he did as it was some miles out.

Alipore was a very different part of Calcutta to that which I had seen before. Rather like one of the wealthier suburbs outside London, and the houses and gardens filled with gorgeous plants and flowers. Here lived the wealthy Indian families and the British Burra Sahibs. Here, too, was a large population of servants, as the higher the man's position, the more servants he had to employ. Not that the employers wished it, but was decided by the senior servants themselves.

It was many years since I had seen my cousin and I didn't know what to expect. Bobs Irwin was the Chief Mechanical Engineer for the Bengal Assam Railway. This was the line that served the 14th Army, so when the Japs invaded Burma, the army suggested to him that he joined them with the rank of colonel, but he turned down the offer as he realised that he would have more authority if he stayed a civilian. For his War-work, he was later awarded the C.I.E. When we passed through Calcutta in August they had been away on local Leave in the Hills. What a difference it would have made to our journey up to Panitola if they had been there. At least they could have told me where we were going and what conditions to expect. Vera would probably have checked our train reservations, and warned us to get there at least one hour beforehand.

At last we arrived at what for me, after the hospital, seemed a very grand house. The Irwins gave me a wonderful welcome, and invited the American in for a drink. It was 10 p.m. and they had almost given up my arrival for that day, but, in spite of this a delicious dinner was served me by their kitmagar – or head servant. Vera had apologised that I would have to have Bob's dressing room, and then later ushed me into a room as big as our five hut rooms combined. And, what bliss, a bath room with real taps running hot and cold water.

In her letters, Vera had warned me that I would have to look after myself by day, as she helped to run a canteen for our troops. She took her job very seriously and worked at it all year round. In spite of this, her house ran smoothly, for she understood Indian servants, and they respected her. She had a good staff of nine, all told, for house and garden, plus two extra bearers for the two men billeted on them.

Next morning she took me aside and told me that they were worried as to the way I had arrived. "You must never accept lifts from strange men," she said. "There are some funny stories going around." But she laughed when I explained that I really couldn't have had a better introduction than through one of his own generals – though if it came to that, the General had been a stranger too! However just to calm her worries, I rang up my kindly American escort and very tactfully turned down his invitation to lunch one day. So what with Matron's rule and Vera's fussing, I never did get taken out by an American.

However that didn't really matter as I soon met up with old friends and my time was fully booked in a little social whirl. What joy to get out of uniform, and wear sleeveless long evening dresses again.

I had plenty to do, starting with a hair perm, my first morning. This had been booked for me with a French hairdresser who was in such demand that she could lay down her own conditions to her clients. I had to wash my own hair at home, and then arrive by taxi at her shop with it wrapped up in a towel. I was also shocked at the rudeness that she showed her clients, from whom she must have made a small fortune. While doing my hair, she talked French to an assistant, and said some horrid things about "the stupid cow" in the next cubicle. I didn't dare show that I understood in case she did something awful to my hair, with which in the end she did a very good job, and it felt heaven to have it looking nice.

That first afternoon, I went on to visit our two old patients who were in the British Military Hospital there. I found the Officers' ward and asked the Sister's permission to visit them. "Oh! You are from their last hospital are you?" she said. "They will be pleased to see you, as they never stop telling us how much better everything was there."

She took me first to the Major, who said, "Thank goodness you've come. I've got two bed-sores, and haven't been comfortable since I arrived."

Sister raised her eyes to heaven with a "You see what I mean" look, and left us. He was much better physically. Perhaps that was why he grumbled so, as he was frustrated at not being able to get about. Old patients can be a perfect nuisance when they move wards. Nothing is ever the same as their old one where they were really ill, and so special patients. Now, having moved hospital, this was all doubly bad. Here they were in a big efficient Base Hospital, with a large staff that came and went with off-duties, and half-days and even days off. He, and David "the stomach" had been very ill indeed for the first few weeks with us, and so became very special patients. They had both been with us for two and a half months, and had got used to having Sister Baptie and myself looking after them all seven days a week. They also had the devoted help from their fellow-officers. Now they were just two more casualties from the Burma Front. Still, no one had had a bed-sore on our ward, so perhaps he had some right to grumble.

I went on to David in the Junior Officers' ward, and heard the same sort of complaints including "and do you know, they even let a V.A.D. do my dressing."

I put a stop to that with, "and what do you think I am?" He turned quite pale. I don't know if it was more the awful mistake he had made, or at the thought of the awful dangers he had been in under my hands. It was fun seeing them and I went twice again. The last time was on my return from Dehra Dunn when they really seemed to be settling in more happily.

David amused Sister Baptie by writing after my first visit, saying that he had hardly recognised me as I looked so glamorous. If he thought that I looked glamorous in a pre-war cotton dress, whatever must we have looked like on the wards?

I met some old friends from Poona days who gave me a good time round Calcutta including dances at both "The Saturday" and "The 400" Clubs. I also got in touch with an old family friend who was stationed there and he arranged to meet me at Firpos restaurant for lunch. Patients had often said how difficult it was to talk to English girls on leave, and that they only got cut dead if they did. But it was difficult for us girls too, as there were so many men and we weren't out to be picked up. On arriving at Firpos, I didn't recognise Robert at the entrance, as he had shaved his moustache and looked quite different. He got some amusement in watching my arrival – the effect any single girl would have had. I had already turned down two offers of lunch and was feeling horribly embarrassed, before the brute came up to greet me. But it served him right, as I still didn't recognise him, until in desperation, he put his hand on my arm and said my name. It was fun seeing him again, and talking of our homes in England. I was able to ask him to dinner at the Irwins.

Finally, one day he saw me off at Howrah station on "The Dunn Express" to my other cousins at Dehra Dunn. "Express" was hardly the right description, but for anyone not in a hurry it was a comfortable and fascinating way to see India. We chugged slowly across the plains for forty-two hours. As there was no buffet car, we stopped at stations for passengers to have their meals. The train just waited until we had finished eating. The guard saw us safely back on board again and off we went. At each station, there were the different restaurants. Those for Mohammedans, Hindus and English style food. I had started the journey with a Ladies Only, two-berth Coupe to myself, but was soon joined by two army sisters. Unfortunately they got out at Bareilly where a lieutenant, his wife and dog got in. Before we could shut the door, a brigadier, his wife and a mountain of luggage pushed their way in and none of us dared to try and stop them. The young wife and I shared the top bunk for my second night while the others sat below. The brigadier had piled their luggage into the lavatory, so that no one could use it. Fortunately, he got out before the situation became really desperate.

On arrival, I must have looked a little weary, for I was promptly put on a bottle of tonic and fed on the most nourishing food for the next two weeks. It was a quiet but wonderfully refreshing holiday, and Dehra Dunn a very pretty semi-hill station. At the end of the fortnight, I was ready for the journey back, which for once was quite easy and uneventful.

Robert, in the meantime, had done his best to get me an air-flight back up to Dinjan. This was not such an easy business as the planes went up filled with freight for China – neither did he have any American connections. But he did get me a preliminary interview with Air Transport, and after seventy minutes of being interviewed by higher and higher officers, I eventually got a place on a transport plane flying up the next day, which was allowed to take some extra weight – me – as far as Dinjan airfield.

I had done a lot of shopping and bought an extra little tin trunk to hold it. I had had a lovely leave and the Irwins had been so very kind and helpful to me. No letters were ever forwarded from the hospital, in case of getting lost, and by now I was ready to go back and see the others again.

This second air-flight turned out to be very different from my first. Just one other passenger and me. We perched on a bench at the side of the plane as the middle was full of oil drums. Fortunately, there was a lavatory in the tail of the plane, as the air smelt so of oil that we were both very sick. I don't think we even spoke to each other as we were both so miserable. Luckily the wind was with us and the flight only took three hours instead of the four hours coming down, and it was certainly better than that awful journey by train.

On arrival at Dinjan, I found an excited Harry waiting for a plane to Calcutta. He said that he and Dorothy were engaged and that he was off to buy the ring. "By the way," he said, "the hospital is packed up and ready to move in forty-eight hours." And he added, "The married girls are all having babies and Matron is furious."

I remembered to congratulate Harry, but could hardly wait for transport to get me to the hospital and hear all that was going on.

On arrival back, I quickly found Verity. Yes, it was true, she was having a baby and was now over two months pregnant. She had no news of Peter, except that he was in the fighting and the news of the battle of Mandalay had been in the paper for some time. Marian had gone on leave to her doctor husband and had not returned – just a certificate of pregnancy was sent to Matron. Penny had come back from her honeymoon and soon, too, was pregnant, and had left to join her husband. All three of these girls were having babies. Our Commandant must have been right that there was something special about tropical nights! It would have been funny if it hadn't affected poor Verity who was the only one on whom Matron could vent her displeasure.

Poor Verity. At first when the nice doctor at St Lukes Mission Hospital had confirmed that she was pregnant, she had had a feeling of panic. Knowing that Peter was in the fighting, she had steeled herself that she might never see him again. But now she had his baby to look after, and she was terrified that she might lose that too.

A Gurkha officer friend of Peter's, a peace-time planter, was now with an I.S.L.U. nearby, and had promised to keep an eye on her. So it was to 'Gaffer' Hayward that she went to ask for advice. Matron had offered to post her back to India, but she dreaded the journey on her own. At Panitola she was at least among friends, and it would be there that the first news of Peter would come. Gaffer calmed her down. He explained again how now she belonged to Peter's regiment, and they would look after her. She must write to them straight away telling them the news and asking for their help. Posts to Dharamsala, where the HQ was took at least a week. But she must have patience, and when eventually they would send for her, he would travel with her at least as far as Calcutta.

So by the time I arrived back, Verity was quietly happy, though still worried and helpless as to her future. She also had evening sickness, and couldn't face dinner at night. Not that Army rations, which were mainly bully beef, were much good for a pregnant mother.

"Since my first non-arrival I have been nothing but a nuisance to Matron," she told me. "Now she just looks on me as a dead loss."

Apart from this, the Sisters' Mess was in the depths of gloom, and the hospital empty. Everyone sat around looking depressed. We had been proud of our hospital, – "The best little hospital in Northern Assam" – and had identified ourselves with the fighting and the 36 Division in particular. It seemed cruel to turn us into a Base Hospital, and to move us to a backwater thirty miles away. We felt cut off from the action and knew little of what was going on. It wasn't until after the war that I read that on 1st April, 36 Division had been returned to General Slim's command. He said in his book what a wonderful job they had done in gaining the admiration and respect of the Americans who had also been fighting under General Stilwell's command. The Americans gave them a great farewell when they turned towards Maymyo to rejoin the rest of the 14th Army. By now it was beginning to be a race to recapture Rangoon, either by seaborne invasion, or by our 14th Army fighting down the length of Burma. The Japanese rarely surrendered, so that it was very bloody fighting all the way. Their casualties were now flown out to hospitals in Southern Assam.

This meant that from now on, only one hospital was needed in our area, and as we were "static" then it must be us. However, the powers that be decided that it would be better if we were at Dibrugarh, thirty miles away. The hospital there was 49 I.G.H.C., and was "mobile" with all furniture collapsible, so they were to be posted forward and we were to take their place. Needless to say, the packing up, which I missed, had been a mammoth job consisting of furniture, electric light bulbs, sign-posts, everything movable including the smart new iron gates that had been put up for the Sister's Mess. For the last week Panitola hospital had been 'ready to move' in forty-eight hours, but it was another ten days before we did. In all, it took a month to pack up and move, and another seven weeks for 49 I.G.H. to leave Dibrugarh.

Most of our patients had been moved by ambulance, over thirty miles of road so bumpy that the surgeon had refused to allow one to travel, as he had a fractured leg strung up on a beam. Instead, an ingenious and successful move was planned for him. As a single track railway passed our hospital, a hand-operated railway trolley was provided with two men to operate it. Our patient, bed and all, was lifted on to a trailer attached behind. Four orderlies went with him, one holding a sunshade over the patient's head, while an ambulance kept pace at the side with all medical comforts. He went off in great style and, as he was the centre of attention the whole way, he thoroughly enjoyed himself and the journey was a great tonic. I had found that there was never a dull moment when travelling in India, but this was something new again.

The day I started back on duty he was still there plus a very few other patients. Officer's ward was empty, except for one patient in a side-ward near the theatre. He was Captain Hodson, one of our older and kindly, British doctors. That day a warning had been given to the hospital staff from an American unit nearby. One of their black G.I.s had committed a murder, a rather ghastly one. He was now on the loose and, as he had been wounded while escaping, the Americans warned us that he might approach any hospital to get First-aid. In fact we were all to keep a look-out and make an immediate report if we saw anyone suspicious: as he could be a very dangerous man.

On my return, Sister Baptie had greeted me with "You're back on 'Officers'. Just regard yourself as part of the equipment," which was her way of paying me a compliment. So when I went on duty at 5 p.m. I was happy to go back to my old ward, and the Indian staff that I knew. The warning about the American murderer didn't worry me at all, in spite of the big ward being empty. I unlocked the kitchen cupboard and got out the electric ring, on which we heated kettles, and soon settled down with a pot of tea to catch up with letter writing. Apart from giving Captain Hodson his medicines and seeing to his supper, I had nothing else to do.

At 8 p.m. I returned to the Mess, and during dinner

remembered that I hadn't locked up the electric ring again. I'd have to go back. Baptie would be furious if it got stolen that night. Dorothy offered to go with me but, surprised, I answered, "No I'll be all right."

When I went back to the hospital, taking my usual short cut across the railway line and in by a side gate, I realised why Dorothy had offered to come too. The usual friendly chatter from the hospital had gone and now there was an eerie silence, and few lights to be seen. As usual, I held my lantern out in front of me to make sure that there were no snakes, and then suddenly I spotted a man scrambling up from the ground ahead. He stood up and his face looked frighteningly dark, for I remembered the warning about the black G.I. He raised his hands and I was too scared to scream, as I thought I would be strangled. Then his hands came together and, "Salaam, Sister Sahib," he said. With relief, I realised that I'd disturbed a nightwatchman just settling down to sleep.

I hurried on to the ward, found the precious heater, and locked it safely away. Then I saw a light from Captain Hodson's room and went in and poured out my tale. He, too, had been warned about this man and he listened quietly and calmed me down. Later, I realised what a rotten Nurse I'd been. There my patient was, ill and all alone, and my fright couldn't have helped his night's sleep.

Next day, we were all thankful when the news came that the man had been caught and was safely locked away.

A few evenings later I went with some others to the Panitola Club for the weekly cinema and dance. While watching the film, I noticed that a good looking captain was looking at us rather than the screen. Later, when the dancing started, Mrs Finlayson came over with this same officer and introduced him. He was a good dancer and we danced together quite often that evening. He told me that in peace-time he was a Ceylon tea-planter, and because of this had been attached to the Pioneer Corps to work on the Imphal Road, and that his company had been in the seige of Imphal. He now had a few days before flying into Burma again via Mykitkyina. Bob asked if he could see me again, and I suggested that he should call into our Mess next evening.

But next day, much of the hospital furniture was to be moved to Dibrugarh. As I had missed all the packing up, Matron told me to go with the stuff from Officers' ward and see that it didn't get muddled up. When everything was settled in, I should go to the Matron of 49 and ask for an ambulance to bring me back. So off I went in the front of a lorry and with an R.A.M.C. Corporal in charge of the rest. We arrived and there was the usual turmoil and noise with all the sepoys shouting at once. The hospital was in process of reconstruction and some new wards being built, and I was told to move Officers' ward into one of these. It was late in the afternoon before I got all the beds and furniture into place, then I went to the Sisters' Mess and reported to Matron.

This was the first time that I had met Miss Sherbourne, the most human and kindly of Matrons. To my surprise she said, "Nurse, it will be dark before you get back. I think you'd better stay the night here. We have a dance on in our Mess and you'd be very welcome, and our V.A.D.s would lend you a change of clothes."

I answered "No," as I was expected back. Yet she insisted that she could telephone our hospital and send a message over to Matron.

"I never let my nurses travel unescorted," she said.

However, I told her that there was an corporal with me and she reluctantly agreed, and ordered an ambulance for us. While waiting for it, she invited me in to have some tea.

Of course, Miss Sherbourne was quite right, for it got dark and then we ran out of petrol. The driver went off with an empty petrol can and we waited in the ambulance at the side of the road. I had never been nervous of Indians walking alone between wards on night duty, but the corporal with me obviously was. He was responsible for me and had no wish for any heroics on my behalf. If it wasn't for his fear, I wouldn't have worried. We kept silence and listened to the pad-pad of feet going by. It seemed a long time before our driver got back, and off we went again.

In the meantime, Bob had arrived at the Mess, written his name on the guard's slate and Dorothy had invited him in for a drink to wait for me. He had heard about the dance at Dibrugarh and knew that I had gone there for the day. So, after waiting an hour, he decided that I had stood him up, and he had left. When at last I returned, tired and hot, it was to find him gone.

The following Saturday, Mrs Findlayson had a celebration tennis party for Dorothy and Harry's engagement, and I went along with them to it. Bob was there, but I hardly spoke to him except to ask why he hadn't waited for me, and I didn't expect to see him again.

9

At last the big day came for us to move and my letters home made it sound like a bit of a nightmare. It was very hot weather and in forty-eight hours we had to change over every bit of equipment with the other hospital, and, at the same time, take over 400 patients. So it wasn't surprising if at times tempers got frayed.

The V.A.D.s from 49. had all been posted to other hospitals, so our Sisters were able to move into their rooms. However, there was no room for us so we took over an empty ward in the hospital. The Medical Officers were also homeless and slept in another ward, but they set up a temporary dining room which they invited us to share. Their cooking and catering was much better than ours, and we were happy to put up with the discomfort.

We slept in a row of camp beds with mosquito nets strung up on wires above. There was no furniture, and we lived out of our boxes. Our camp baths and basins were put out in the empty dressings room, and there was a row of thunderboxes in the office. Our private bearer had come with us, and was invaluable in organising everything. Those who were off duty in the afternoon just lay or sat on their beds. About 4 p.m. one of us would order baths and they would be filled up. Then the bearer would banish himself and the other servants to a safe distance and forgetting all modesty, we would sit in the baths communally, and chatter while we washed. Then we would dress, be off to tea in the M.O.s dining room, and on duty at 5 p.m.

When three new sisters were posted to the hospital, there were no rooms for them in the Mess, so they were sent down to join us. We felt rather sorry for them as they had come straight from a comfortable hospital in India. One had even been an assistant matron, but we stopped feeling sorry for her when, on her second day, and the baths were ready, she suddenly announced, "I am going to have a bath and I expect privacy." She then shut the door on our astonished faces and we were left to get dressed all hot and sticky.

However, the move over, an official notice came in asking everyone if they wished to be posted forward. We V.A.D.s were delighted and promptly all signed "Yes," whereas the Q.A.s of both hospitals had all been out some years and had had enough, and all signed "No." So there was a big re-organisation of staff and sadly most of our Sisters were posted back to India, while new ones arrived in their places. I never did learn who belonged to where, and the whole thing must have been absolute hell for the two matrons. After a couple of weeks there was a big clear-out, and then we V.A.D.s were given a room each in the Sister's Mess. However, Verity shared one with me as by then she was waiting for an order to join Peter's Regimental HQ.

I, myself, only had a week of this ward life, as I started on my second night duty. I moved up to the night sister's quarters but still had my meals in the M.O.s Mess, so I had a rather difficult and lonely two weeks. An early dinner served me by myself, and then breakfast with the doctors at which we none of us felt inclined to talk. If Verity was off duty in the evenings, she would come up to see me, but the others were mostly out.

The Indian side of the hospital was much larger than the British, so the night duty HQ was in the little bamboo office in the middle of a block of four Major Medical wards. Being lit by electric light, we were very conspicuous from the darkness outside, and so never had a chance of a snooze. Besides this, in front of us was a hand-pump which supplied water for these wards.

The Hindu religion tells them to wash all over every day, and so, from about 4.30 a.m. on, there would be a shadowy line of patients working the pump and washing underneath it, with just loincloths on. Their washing always included a great clearing of the throat and a spitting. The noise from 120 patients was terrific, but the bed-patients, of course, just spat on the floor.

One of the nursing sepoys would boil us some tea, and I mean boil. He had a kettle of cold water to which he added a handful of tea leaves, and then heated it to boiling over an oil stove by the pump. At first I thought that I would never be able to drink it, but at 5 a.m. we needed something strong, and it certainly was that. I think that, as a concession to us, he poured it through some hospital gauze to strain off the tea leaves.

My special charge were these four Indian Medical wards where there were a suprising number of pneumonia and chest cases. They were on penicillin injections or sulphonamide tablets, and I had to see that their nursing sepoys stayed awake and did their jobs properly. The Little Monsoon broke and it rained for five days and nights, so the wards were full and the coughing and spitting horrendous.

I was thankful that my mother had sent me out my rubber boots as there were no connections between some of the wards, or between the Sisters' Mess and the hospital. So for five nights we paddled around and floundered into puddles in the dark. One of the wards was flooded, a minor one fortunately, and great was the wailing and crying before the patients could be moved. There were cows in the compound around, which was perhaps why there were no leeches, for which I was very thankful.

Night Sister did the rounds of the hospital and also the three-hourly penicillin injections, and in between times she sat with me in the office. Sister X was an unhappy, frustrated woman with no interests outside the hospital, and had been out in the forward areas for a long time. This must have been the beginning of her third Hot-weather, and everything had got her down. I had had little contact with her at Panitola, but I felt that she disliked me, though thought no more of it. I didn't realise how deep was her resentment – or what a sour bitch she could be.

When we moved to Dibrugarh she had been put straight on to night duty and was full of the trials and difficulties she had had, while taking over from the sisters of 49. I soon got tired of hearing her tales of the other hospital's sisters who just sat around criticising, while we of Panitola had to do all the work.

My first night on, and early in the morning when everything was at its worst, a patient died. The nursing sepoy drew back the mosquito net and left him for me to see, as no Caste Hindu would touch a dead body either human or animal. They had one of their own Untouchables who was sent for when there was a man to be laid out. Now, without a mosquito net around him, the man's face and neck were covered with mosquitoes that were gorging on his blood, and I found the sight loathsome and revolting.

When Sister returned from her rounds I reported the man's death.

"Why aren't you laying him out?" she asked.

"But we don't lay out Hindu patients," I answered, surprised.

"What do you mean by telling me what to do," she said furiously. "A good nurse always lays out her own patients, and I expect the same of you."

"But, Sister, they have their own customs," I faltered.

"Well, if you don't know how then I will help you with him. Now hurry up and do as I say."

So together we worked on the man, while the nursing sepoy and other patients watched in silent disapproval.

I had had no sleep the day before, working until 1 p.m. and then moving up to my new room, so I went off duty feeling both physically and emotionally exhausted. I couldn't eat anything at breakfast, and when I noticed sympathetic glances from the doctors, I drank up my tea and left. For both British and Indian M.O.s would have been shocked that Hindu customs had been ignored, and if I had said anything I would only have dissolved into tears. So I took a large sleeping draught and went to bed.

Next evening Sister was more pleasant, and might even have realised how wrong she had been. "I think you had better start each evening on Officers ward," she said. "You can help the orderly settle them for the night. After all you won't be happy off Officers', will you?" she added with a snide aside. But we got on all right from then on, settling down into a dull routine.

During the night my main job was to do tours of our four Indian Medical wards, and they had quite an assortment of patients. 'Puggle' is an Urdu word meaning mad. But it was a useful one for describing anyone who was at all peculiar or, as in one ward, it described an epileptic. Once on shining my lantern through his mosquito net I saw that he was having a fit. There were implements beside him in case this should happen, but never had I had to use them before. Quickly I pulled the net up, and forcing an instrument between his jaws, I then pulled his tongue forward with the forceps. It wasn't much of a compliment that he should throw a fit on the sight of me, but I felt pleased that I had managed to cope so quickly by myself.

There were three other patients that the sepoys described as 'Puggle', and I never really knew what they were meant to do. One night on coming on duty I found one of them strapped down to his bed, and I began to wonder who would go puggle next.

At 6 a.m. the three nursing sepoys started their washing rounds of the very ill patients. I had a running battle with them over this as I found that they each used the same flannel and basin of water for all the patients in each ward. Finally I made a truly British compromise, and only insisted that they change the water and flannel every three patients. Even so, they thought me very fussy. Apart from these wards we weren't at all busy as the hospital was only half full, and few patients very ill. However, Sister was conscientious and went regularly on her rounds. I filled in the time writing long letters and catching up with my correspondence.

A nice thing had happened. A letter arrived from David – "the stomach" – who wrote to thank me for visiting him in Calcutta. He said that he was now up and off to a Convalescent Home, prior to repatriation back to England. He then went on to write a lovely letter of thanks to Sister Baptie and myself for what we had done for him at Panitola. It is always nice to be thanked, but this was a wonderfully worded token of affectionate gratitude. I only wish that I had kept it, for it certainly cheered me and helped me to feel that everything was worth while.

After seven days, the sisters changed and the new one was a stranger. I don't know where she came from, but suspected that she was a bad egg passed on to us by 49. Hospital. I never saw her again after night duty so perhaps Matron, too, posted her swiftly on. She too had been out too long, but she was younger and had lost all interest in the hospital and gone man-mad. There was a patient in Officers' ward that she took a great fancy to.

"Do you like him?" she asked me.

"No, I don't," I said. "I think he might be a rather horrid type."

"Oh! You don't know how to have a bit of fun. I do, and I am going to meet him this evening. Do you mind being a dear and doing my penicillin injections for me at twelve?" she asked. It was then that I realised that, if I agreed, I might not see her for hours. "No, I'm sorry," I answered quickly. "V.A.D.s don't do penicillin injections, and I don't think I'd know how to do one."

She looked annoyed but there was nothing she could do about it. However, to give her her due, she turned up promptly at twelve o'clock each night, but then disappeared again until 3 a.m., when she returned for the next injections. I didn't mind doing the Rounds for her, as it got me out into the fresh air and gave me something to do. Though I did wonder what Matron Davis, of Aldershot, would say if she knew one of her old V.A.D.s was in charge of a whole hospital for several hours each night – but if she could have seen my rubber boots and swinging lantern, she might have smiled!

On arrival at an Indian block of wards, I would be greeted by "Salaam, Sister Sahib," whereas on the British side there would be a friendly, "Evenin' Nurse." While on Officer's, the orderly gave me a wink to show that he knew just why I was there instead of Sister.

If there had been an accident, or other crisis, I wouldn't have hesitated in sending for an M.O. and so showing her up. But nothing happened, and it wasn't until the end of the week that Matron heard what was going on. The patient was discharged, and Sister sat in the office looking sulky, as to begin with she was quite sure that it was I who had split on her. As I said before, at the end of the Night-duty she was posted away from the hospital, and the story well hushed up.

Then a second nice thing happened for, to my surprise, a parcel of magazines arrived with a note from Bob. He said that he had a new posting near Dibrugarh, and might he call on me? So I replied asking him in to the Mess for a drink one evening about 6 p.m. He came next day and later arranged to take me out for lunch on my Day-off after Night-duty. I was pleased, too, to have the magazines to read, while sitting by myself in that lonely office.

By now the rains had stopped and the skies were clear and dry. There was great excitement one evening when an outdoor cinema was set up and a film in Urdu shown for the Indian patients, and so when I arrived on duty, it was to find an almost empty ward. Looking at the report I saw that there should be nine seriously ill patients in bed, but only four of them were there. They had all gone out to the cinema and there was nothing that I could do about it but wait until they returned, and hope that they would be none the worse for it. Actually they weren't; all having had a lovely time, they slept the better for it that night.

Unless they were really very ill, Indian patients would always get up to watch any excitement that was going on. Once, when a visiting general was inspecting the hospital, he was taken into a side-ward to be shown a man who was supposed to be very ill and an interesting case. To the horror of Matron and the M.O.s, there was no patient there. He was outside, sitting on his hunkers on the verandah, watching the General's Round!

I was thankful when the two weeks were up and I moved into the room that Verity and I were to share, though the hut was bare compared to that at Panitola, and there was no verandah to shade the sun from its bamboo walls. Verity was now on a Minor Indian ward where there wouldn't be much physical work to be done, but she felt very tired by the evening and was frequently sick. The nursing sepoys were kind, and brought her bowls to the office to be sick into, and then emptied them themselves, and did all they could to save her work. It seemed cruel of Matron to keep her working, but probably sensible to give her an occupation to stop her from worrying, for she still hadn't heard either from Peter or his HQ.

I lunched with Bob at a Chinese restaurant, and it was a pleasure to sit and talk quietly after the strain of the last two weeks. Then he drove me to the bazaar where I bought some material to be made up into curtains and covers for my room, and which would soon make it more homely. Everyone knew what everyone else was doing in Dibrugarh and we girls were conspicuous, so I wasn't surprised to be waved at by old friends or patients.

That evening I went to dinner with Peter Church, at Sub Area H.Q. He was very excited as he was going home on repatriation and, being a popular officer, had been on a big round of farewell parties. He was gloriously happy but, perhaps because of all those many celebrations, I thought he looked slightly the worse for wear!

Budge Birket, the Major in charge of Labour units, spoke teasingly to me saying, "I saw you out this afternoon, so I gather you are the reason that I've had to change all my postings around."

"What do you mean?" I asked.

Well, Bob is a friend of mine from Ceylon. He recently came to me saying that it was about time someone else had a front-line posting, and that he would like to be in this area. Actually I owed him a favour. For when he first arrived he helped me out with some trouble in one of our units. They were a Tamil speaking lot, and their officer only spoke Urdu. So, as I knew Bob was fluent in Tamil, I sent him along and he soon got things sorted out."

This was all interesting news indeed.

10

On starting duty next morning I found that I was to be on the Indian Major Surgical block of three wards, which were now run by Sister X. When I arrived she looked no more pleased to see me than I was to be there, but for a few days we got on all right and our duties were opposite each other on the afternoon shifts.

At Panitola there were no facilities for giving Blood Transfusions, but here at 49. I.G.H. it was possible, though everyone wondered quite how reliable they were. A morning came when our Surgeon ordered a transfusion for a patient. Sister X. set it all up, and on leaving at one p.m. she gave me instructions for watching it. Back in Aldershot they had become almost routine, and I had often helped with them and knew that if ever a patient should show a change in his condition, it meant that the wrong blood grouping had been given. Very soon this man started an uncontrolled shivering, and certainly the blood seemed to be doing him no good. The surgeon was operating in the theatre and so it was up to me to make a decision straight away, and I turned the transfusion off.

However, when Sister X. came back, she was furious. "How dare you turn it off without my telling you to? Who do you think you are?" I tried to explain about the patient's condition, but she just wouldn't listen and ranted on at me for my behaviour. So there was nothing for it but to walk out and leave her.

Next morning at breakfast, I had a message to go and see Matron, so off I went rather in fear and trembling. To my surprise she greeted me pleasantly, saying that she had some bad news as Sister X. had gone sick with shingles, and was moving into the Mission hospital. "I have two alternatives," Matron said. "Either I can move a sister from the Minor wards, which would disrupt the two blocks instead of one. Or, as I am expecting some new sisters any day now, perhaps you could take charge of these wards in the meantime, if I give you two other V.A.D.s to help you. Do you feel capable of running these three wards?"

"Yes, Matron, I will certainly try," I answered. In fact I was so pleased that Sister wouldn't be there, that I really felt capable of running anything. So Dorothy and a new V.A.D. came to help, and we three managed on our own for ten days. Sadly though, the whisper went round our Mess that Sister didn't have shingles, but a nervous breakdown, and wouldn't be coming back. Poor Sister X. had done wonderful work in the past but now she was a War casualty as much as any of the men back from the Front-line.

Each morning I took the ward report to Matron and was able to tell her that all was well but, as there were some bad fractures with big dressings to be done, I asked Major Ghosh, the Surgeon, to come and watch me while I did them. He was very pleased to advise and also a great help to me in the general running of the ward.

There was a lot of office work; everything to be carefully ordered and counted including the right number of Hindu and Mohammedan meals each day; the medicine cupboard kept locked, and a tally of all drugs going out. So different to the casual way we had managed on Officers' ward. The rum ration also had to be given out to the Hindus and cigarettes for everyone but the Sikhs.

Three bottles of disinfectant were to be ordered daily from the Dispensary to help clean the floors after the patients spat on them. When the sweeper was going to wash a ward floor, he brought the bucket along and I tipped a bottle of disinfectant in, and this he repeated for the other two wards. He was a good and intelligent sweeper and also a born nurse. If the patients wanted help, they always preferred to call him rather than one of the nursing sepoys. Matron and several sisters had tried to get permission for him to be sent off for nursing training, but each time the request was turned down. Major Ghosh explained it to me saying that as he was "an untouchable", no Caste Hindu would work with him as a nursing sepoy. He had been born a sweeper and could never rise above it, however intelligent or hard working he was.

Penicillin injections were now becoming almost routine and

we had several patients on them. I and the other V.A.D.s soon got used to giving them and thought nothing of it, but I always felt sorry for the poor patients. A painful injection every three hours, day and night, was an exhausting as well as a painful business. They had hardly got to sleep at night before they were woken up again. Our ward owned the only refrigerator in the hospital, so penicillin stocks had to be kept for the other wards as well, and every three hours they sent over for it. We had always been told what a wonder drug it was and I soon had a demonstration of this.

The V.D. ward didn't have any Sisters or V.A.D.s and one of the patients was prescribed a course of penicillin. Their doctor asked if I would house the patient on our verandah and give him his injections, but his own ward would both feed and look after him themselves. I duly gave him his course of jabs and, after the last one, told him to return to his ward. He got up and gave a deep salaam of gratitude right down to the ground at my feet. I was astonished. It turned out that he had been carried in as a stretcher case and now, to him, it really seemed a miracle cure.

Soon after, another man salaamed to my feet, but in desperate petition for, in one of the wards, I had noticed that a patient always had a visitor with him, and after a bit I told this man to go home. The next day he was still there, so I got annoyed and told him to leave, at which he fell at my feet and started sobbing. We girls were very innocent and I didn't know about homosexuality. I did think that there was something funny going on, and sent for the Orderly Sergeant.

Instead of taking the man away, he gave him a cigarette and sat down to talk to him. I was furious, and said so. "Steady on, Nurse," said the sergeant. "This is really nothing. Just leave us, and I will deal with them." The man was moved to an Indian hospital and the subject explained to me by someone. However, I didn't forget my shock and revulsion at seeing this man crying at my feet.

Major Ghosh was a wonderful kindly doctor to all the patients. But this was not the case with some of the juniors who acted as Orderly Medical Officers. I had a spot of bother with one young M.O. who thought that most of my patients were too low caste for him to be troubled with. I was very annoyed when one evening a patient was brought in unconscious from Casualty, without a word on his papers to say what was wrong.

I sent for this M.O. who, after about ten minutes, strolled up. He was surprised that I was worried for, as he said, "He is an IS.LU. coolie. They are very strong. He will soon recover, so don't you worry Sister."

I had had a hot and tiring day, and the strain of running the three wards on my own was beginning to tell. I took the M.O. into the office and speaking in English which none of the ward staff could understand, I told him just what I thought of him. "He may be just an IS.LU. coolie to you, but to me he is a patient to be looked after," I ended.

He had every right to be furious with me, for nurses don't tell doctors what to do, nor should they speak to them rudely. But I think some of the Indian doctors looked on us British sisters and nurses as a race slightly apart, rather like missionaries – eccentric and a little foolish that we bothered so with the low caste patients. To my surprise he didn't take umbrage, and in fact he apologised to me. Afterwards he couldn't have been nicer, taking great trouble over this patient, who did, as he had said, recover very quickly. Nor did he ever show me any sign of ill will.

We were now under Indian Command and the Indian doctors were allowed to have their wives with them. Mrs Ghosh had arrived, and the Major asked us three V.A.D.s to come and have a cup of tea with them one evening and meet her. It was kind of him, both to ask us and to allay her curiosity about us. She was sweet, but very shy, as she was of the generation that had been brought up in purdah (which meant seeing no men, but those of her family) and anyway, not to speak in company with her husband present. She must have thought us very strange, forward, young women the way we chatted and talked to her husband though we were his equal. It was a kind thought of his to ask us and we enjoyed meeting her. British women have often been criticised for holding aloof from the Indians, but it was rather a case of fifty-fifty, as we were brought up in such different ways, and the Indian women did not always want to join us. Later, when I was with my cousins in Calcutta they had a very cheerful luncheon party for Bobs Irwin's Indian colleagues. However, none of the men brought their wives, and Vera and I were the only women present.

Soon we had a great surprise. We seven V.A.D.s were to be attached to 49. I.G.H. and move forward with them, and the word went round that it was eventually to be Rangoon. We were delighted. Our old Sisters, including Baptie, had already been posted away, and the C.M.H. had become a very different place. Miss Sherbourne, their Matron, took the trouble to interview us each separately. To me she asked, "Are you taking your Mepacrine tablets regularly?"

This was because a few months before, a Command Order had come out that all ranks of the 14th Army were to go on a new anti-malaria tablet called Mepacrine, and these we had to take regularly every day. For women they could have side effects, and also turned everyone into a jaundiced shade of yellow. I had been bitten so many times by mosquitoes on my first night duty that I decided that I must be immune to malaria. Anyway, I was planning to go off on leave in February and had no wish to look bright yellow. So I didn't take them, and nobody bothered to ask if we did. When I returned from my month's leave, it was to find everyone very jaundiced looking. I stood out a mile with my pale complexion and Miss Sherbourne must have wondered for some time.

"No, Matron," I said, stammering my feeble excuse.

"I see, Nurse, but remember, if you want to come with us to Rangoon, and I hope you will, then you must take Mepacrine regularly." She never asked me again. She didn't have to, as I turned as yellow as anyone.

I was extra pleased at the thought of leaving, for now Verity had gone. At long last she had heard from Peter's HQ welcoming her to Dharumsala, and telling her to start on the long train journey across India. True to his word, Gaffer Hayward arranged an airflight down to Calcutta in an American plane for all three of them. He couldn't take her further himself, but was sending his capable Indian orderly with her all the way, to help her with her luggage. From Calcutta she had a four day train journey to reach Dharumsala. We were all worried for her as it was quite a journey, especially as she was liable to be train sick.

But the unbelievable happened. They went to the Grand Hotel and she walked straight into her husband, Peter. The same incredible coincidence, at the same place. Peter had been in the jungle battles and had only just heard from her about the baby. He had flown to Calcutta to travel up to Dibrugarh the next day. One day earlier and they would have missed each other. So he was able to take his wife on to Dharumsala himself, and see her installed in a bungalow with other officers' wives. She was over four months pregnant, and now she and her baby could be looked after properly. It was a long time for Verity to wait among strangers, but she had the support of other wives whose husbands were in action too. However Peter went back into Burma to fight on down in what was becoming a victorious army, although still a very hard and bloody campaign.

One evening, Bob and I went in a party of six to Panitola Planters' Club. We girls all wore evening blouses and skirts that we had had made from pretty materials we had found in the bazaar. They had long sleeves and skirts to pass the anti-malaria regulations, but were hardly the way to dress for the rain.

On the drive there, it started to pour with rain but luckily we had arrived before the storm (or hurricane as it was officially called later) really got going and became very frightening. Wind, rain, hail, and the tin roof of the Club lifted up and down, while everyone thought that it would go any minute. When the worst was over, we came out to find that the Basha huts around were flattened, and debris everywhere.

We were advised to wait until the roads were cleared, but we girls got worried as to what was happening at our hospital. Chaos must be reigning and everyone would be needed to help. So we started back in two trucks, with Bob and I leading in his – but not for long. The road had fallen away on our left, and not being able to see well through the pouring rain, our front wheel went down and we tipped into the ditch. Luckily the others were behind and saw us in time. We struggled out and across to their truck and Dorothy called out for me to come and sit in front between her and Harry, where I could dry off in the heat from the engine. We were both soaked, and my long skirt dripped around me and never looked the same again.

The journey back was grim, and the thirty miles took three hours. Everywhere was devastation, and through the villages we could hear wailing and the sound of children crying. Trees were down across the road, but the Americans were soon on the job clearing them away. While we waited, we wondered if we would find our own Basha rooms flattened too, and what might have happened to our precious possessions. But as we got nearer, the weather cleared, and we found that Dibrugarh had hardly been touched at all. The centre of the storm had been at Panitola, and it certainly felt like it. Our old hospital lost roofs from several of the wards, and the village suffered badly too. For the first time we were glad that we had been moved to Dibrugarh.

Luckily, just the day before, a replacement Sister had arrived and been given charge of my Indian Surgical wards. We certainly needed her, as IS.LU patients poured in with concussion or fractures of all sorts. For a week or so we were frantically busy, and there was the great feeling again of everyone working their hardest together.

Then I was moved on to the British Medical Block, where I had a very soft and easy job. Four wards, with nineteen patients in all, and none of them very ill. I had four British orderlies to help, and no Sister. The doctor, Captain Hodson, was a nice middle-aged type of R.A.M.C. and had been out for three years. "I don't know why you girls are so excited about moving," he grumbled. "In my experience, I'd say it'll be four months before you get settled again." He wasn't far wrong as it turned out, and it was another four weeks before we moved.

There was very little to do, and four capable orderlies to see to it. I did the rounds in the morning. I asked the dysentery patients, "How many times have you been," and then went round again with the doctor, after which an orderly brought us tea and my work for the day was pretty well over. Still, it was very hot and we had no fan in the office, so I found it difficult not to sit in a stupor, half asleep.

However, we became busy when one morning Captain Hodson came in worried about the new Quartermaster who had been sent up since we came under Indian Command. This officer was out to be a new broom and show just how inefficient everything had been before. What really put him on his mettle was that the last Q.M. had been a woman – a young one at that – so things must surely be in a bad way. She was an English girl who had been brought up in India, and a Captain in the W.A.C.I., who had lived with us in the Sisters' Mess. She understood her job well, and she had been a great help in rush times, supplying everything that she was asked for within reason without stock-taking, and up to now, no one had minded. The M.O.s signed for the equipment of the wards that they were responsible for, though they realised that a lot of the moveable things might be missing.

Captain Hodson had signed for four wardful's of equipment, so naturally was worried. I had a day of checking every item and found that we only had enough of the smaller things for two wards, some for three, and none for the fourth. The doctor was horrified at the thought of the cost it would be to him and there was general consternation. However, our very efficient corporal nursing orderly said, "Don't worry Sir, you just keep out of the way when the Q.M. comes. If Nurse will do as I say, I'll see that we get through all right."

Stock-taking came round and I now feel slightly ashamed of what we did. But I tell it to show the great feeling that there was to protect our W.A.C.I. Captain. The new Q.M. was a regular soldier and, as I have said, quite sure no woman could possibly run a hospital stores, and it was almost an insult to him to think that she could. He came from a Base Hospital in India and just had no idea that all ranks in our hospital would join up together against him in defence of what we considered our own. For he was one of "Them" and the M.O. and the girl belonged to "Us", and he didn't stand a chance.

The Q.M. arrived and he and I moved into Ward 1. He checked everything off as satisfactory, and then we moved into Ward 2. Here, I had to slow him down and keep him talking with his back to the door and the other wards. Over his shoulder I could see the four orderlies rushing across from One to Three with armfulls of equipment – mugs, plates, bowls, buckets, jugs etc. Slowly we moved down the ward and I got him enthusing about the efficiency of his last hospital and the way he liked things done. He hadn't been listened to so attentively for years and his pace from bed to bed become slower and slower. At last at the doorway the corporal gave me the V-sign, so then we were able to move out into Ward 3.

Just then the corporal dashed out of Ward 1 with two water jugs that had been forgotten and were meant for Ward 4. The Q.M. stopped dead and stared but, with great presence of mind, the orderly stopped at the pump and filled them with water and returned to One. The Q.M.s eyes narrowed and he looked thoughtful. He realised that there was something up, and that he was having a very old army trick played on him. He couldn't have guessed how big a trick for he decided to ignore it, and we moved on to Three. Here again, everything was complete. Before long, the corporal again gave me the V-sign and we were able to check the fourth ward. At the end everything was signed as complete. "You seem to have a very efficient lot of orderlies here, Nurse," he said, and I heartily agreed. He knew – and he knew that I knew that he knew.

The Q.M. left and we sent for Captain Hodson and all six had a celebratory cup of tea together. After all, if the man was so efficient, he would soon make up any deficiencies he might find later. Being Wards 1, 2, 3, and 4, we were the first that he had checked. I don't remember what happened in the rest of the hospital, but doubtless, he was more careful from then on. Our nineteen patients had had a wonderful time watching and, in some cases, even helping. It was as good as a pantomime to them, as the poor Q.M.s were never popular members of any unit.

The new wards were at last finished, and we were to move in. The new chemical D.D.T. had arrived for the hospital and the whole place was to be treated with it. A long line of sepoys, wearing masks, flitted the compound and wards. First they did the new blocks. Then we moved the patients across, plus all the beds, furniture and equipment. This, of course, meant a mighty upheaval with much noise and shouting. Then the line of sepoys went right across the old hospital, wards and all. The result was incredible. The evening before the air had buzzed with mosquitoes, now suddenly there were none. We had heard of this amazing new chemical, but never realised how startling the results would be. Incidentally, it was also lethal to bugs in cane chairs, and it was now safe to sit down without spreading a newspaper there first. Someone gave me a tin of insecticide spray. It was like a new toy and I soon used it up chasing insects out of my room.

Our patients were very bored normally, as there was no wireless or library, and very little for them to do. "Housey, Housey", or Bingo as it is now called, was one of their occupations and we soon learned the descriptions of the numbers off by heart. Occasionally they would sing, and of course "A troopship is leaving Bombay" was one of the favourites. There was nothing much wrong with any of them apart from malaria and dysentery for which they had to have long and boring treatments. Their great hope was to be sent home on repatriation. "When are you due for repat.?" was the big topic of conversation. Captain Hodson was in the seventeenth group, but as he was a doctor he was gloomy as to his chances of getting back when due.

Everyone was waiting, both for the end of the war in Europe and for the taking of Rangoon. Fighting was bitter all the way down through Burma and few Japs surrendered. They fought to the finish as it was against their training to give themselves up as prisoners. So, many lives were lost needlessly on both sides. Our patients quietly dreaded being sent back to their units to go on with the endless bloodshed.

I had an easy time by day, so off-duty I was glad to go out most evenings. There were a lot of parties in the units around, mostly for officers going back on repat. I went to many of them with Bob and grew to like him more and more.

One hazard I found were old patients. So many officers had been into our ward at Panitola, if only for a few days, that I was often greeted and spoken to in a friendly way that Bob found annoying. "He is only an old patient," I would say. In the end it became a joke. This happened to all of us and from all ranks. One Sister was hailed from the top of an elephant with a "Salaam Sister Sahib," by the mahout.

We sometimes had dinner at Harry's unit. He had been a Gurkha officer but, like Bob, because he was a tea planter, he had been attached to a Labour Unit, so they had much in common. Harry had a bungalow on the banks of the Brahmaputra, and a motor boat to go with it. The water was too dirty for bathing but we often went out in the boat in the evenings and delighted in the cool air on the river.

There was the evening that Bob asked me to marry him. He couldn't have chosen a more romantic setting with the full moon, the river and the mysterious jungle on the other side. I refused him, explaining how impossible I found it to decide about marrying anyone out there. Our lives were so unnatural and how could either of us know our true feelings. Daily I expected to hear that our hospital was moving on – so I just lived for the present.

The M.O.s had the only wireless in the hospital so kept us posted as to the latest news. On 2nd May, Rangoon was occupied by a seaborne landing force, so the 14th Army had lost the race south by a few days. The Japanese had evacuated the town and on the top of the roof of the local gaol there was written in big letters, "Japs gone. Exdigate," by the R.A.F. prisoners there. An R.A.F. Mosquito pilot crash-landed his plane just north of Rangoon, and then walked in and visited the P.O.W.s. Having made sure that the Japs had really gone, he commandeered a sampan, and sailed down the river to give the news to 26 Division on the ships outside. And so Rangoon was re-occupied by the British and great was the rejoicing in the 14th Army.

8th May was Victory Day over Germany. We were so far away and I wished I could have been in England to join in the exctitement. We felt rather flat in the hospital so the M.O.s threw an impromptu party for us to hear Churchill's speech on the wireless. Really the fall of Rangoon had meant more to us, and now perhaps the hospital might move off.

A few days later, Dibrugarh Club laid on a Victory Party to which we were all asked, including any British up-patients. This meant every patient in my wards, and they went off in two ambulances with one of the number, a sergeant, in charge. By the time I got to the Club later in the evening, most of them were well away at the bar. They weren't used to spirits and the gin went to their heads. There were some good local gins made in India, but there were also some very bad ones. One in particular was nicknamed Dikin Death and it was said that several American servicemen had been returned home blinded by it. Whatever the

Club bearers were serving our patients, it was certainly potent and I dreaded to think what was happening to the insides of our dysentery patients. The sergeant hadn't a hope of stopping them, and nor had I. When eventually the party ended, I counted my lot out to the ambulances, but many of them insisted on travelling on the roofs instead of inside. They went off singing happily. One fell off and broke his ankle, otherwise they all arrived intact.

Dorothy was on night duty, and collected a bunch of my patients who had got lost and took them back across the field that separated the two blocks. She wondered if she was being a fool to go off in the dark with a crowd of drunks, but looking back, was touched to see that her whole staff of three nursing sepoys and a sweeper were all following close behind her as protection. It must have been quite a night for the hospital, as doubtless there was trouble on the surgical side as well.

Next morning, the wards were unrecognisable. The hangovers were terrible, and I had nineteen bed-patients. The orderlies didn't look too good either. When Matron came round, she took the scene in and looked very grim. She certainly had no sympathy for the man whose ankle was by then in plaster. She couldn't actually lay the blame on me, but looked as though she would like to and I really felt as though I was in disgrace.

11

Towards the end of May, 49. I.G.H. (c) at last was posted forward into S.E.A.C. again, but I didn't go with them. For weeks I had been waiting and looking forward to it, and then when the posting arrived I was in bed with a strep. throat and glands and felt terribly disappointed. We were now under the Matron of 49. and she again showed me her real concern for our welfare. She came and told me that she had arranged that I should go into the Mission Hospital until I was fit to travel, and then I was to follow them to the Transit Camp at Chittagong. Our old C.M.H. Matron was being replaced by a new one, and Miss Sherbourne had left instructions that a bearer must accompany me, as she would never allow any of her staff to travel alone.

So I went off by ambulance to St. Luke's and missed the horrendous move south done by the rest of the unit. Miss Sherbourne must have been very thankful to leave at last after two months of hanging around in someone else's Mess, while most of her sisters were posted away and with the prospect of weeks of travel ahead. Still, she was a Regular Q.A. used to the ups and downs of Army life.

They were very kind to me at St. Luke's and put me on sulphonamide tablets. "My gums swelled up and were very sore and I was like a toothless old woman mumbling away at mince and rice pudding – a shame as the food there was so jolly good." Bob, of course, was rather pleased that I had been left behind and was a constant and welcome visitor. When I left, the doctor said that I must see the dentist as my back teeth seemed to be giving trouble.

We had a dentist at the C.M.H. and a British one at that, but he wasn't one of the world's best dentists, as I was to discover. On examining my teeth, he said, "Ah! yes." It was my lower wisdom teeth and he would have them out in no time. He gave me injections and pulled and pulled, while the orderly hung on to my head, and then he pulled and pulled again.

"Oh dear, they are impacted," he said. "I would have done them in the theatre if I'd known. Still, if you can stand it I may as well get them finished."

So he cut and pulled, and cut again, and then gave me another set of injections even further back. My face started swelling visibly and he got worried and fetched the gin bottle. "Would you like a good strong drink of this?" he asked. It was then that I knew that we were really back in the 19th Century dentistry. After forty very long minutes he had both teeth out, and I fairly tottered back to my room and collapsed into bed.

At least he was worried about me, and went and told the Home Sister. There were big holes left which became infected. My face and jaw swelled up and the pain was awful, and up went my temperature again. I asked to go back to St. Luke's but I couldn't as the dentist was giving me treatment each day, packing the holes with penicillin paste. The injections had been so far back that they had done something to my jaw, so that temporarily I couldn't open my mouth to eat, and only sucked in liquid. Luckily our old private bearer was still with me. He sat on his hunkers outside my room and fetched what I asked for, and I was no trouble to them up at the Mess.

Otherwise I was alone all day. It was very hot with the sun beating through the bamboo walls of my hut, nor could I sleep much at night with the pain in my jaws. All together I was so miserable and low with little food and sleep that at the end of a week I just broke down in tears. Then I remembered a bottle of whisky that I had in my suitcase – so I hopped out and drank quite a lot. When Bob came to see me in the evening, I was half-tight, but much better. I had some more before going to sleep and slept well for the first time.

Bob came to see me each evening. I wrote to a girl friend, "Imagine how awful I looked with my face swollen and my hair on end. But he never once showed that he minded, and he said that, to him, I looked just the same. It's perfectly true, that when someone is fond enough of you, it doesn't matter a damn what you look like."

Gradually it all got better and Home Sister said that I was to have three weeks sick leave in Shillong, and she was booking me to stay in the Y.W.C.A. Leave Club. 49. I.G.H. were still at Chittagong, and would be for some time so there was no hurry for me to join them. Three weeks in a hill station. How absolutely wonderful!

Then, out of the blue, came a Movement Order promoting Bob to Major, and to join a Pioneer Unit at Rangoon. This letter was dated 7th May and had only just arrived. The coincidence was incredible. He took ten days' compassionate leave and travelled with me up to Shillong where he stayed for the first half of my leave, and it all turned into a lovely holiday.

The Y.W.C.A. Hostels were set up for us Service girls during the war, and the British women who ran them were truly wonderful in their kindness to us. We took the train as far as Gauhati, where there was a Transit Hostel where I could stay, and where they even found a room for Bob. Next day, we went by bus up into the hills to Shillong. It was heaven to feel the air getting cooler at last, and to see such pretty scenery around. I got a warm welcome at the Leave Club and was put in a room to share with a Sister who was also convalescing. Every morning a good breakfast was brought to us in bed and no hurry to get up. The English woman running it made us all feel as much at home as possible, and the food seemed marvellous.

Bob was at an Officers' Mess nearby but I was allowed to ask him in for any meal that I liked. I hadn't noticed that he had put up his Major's crowns until I heard the R.T.O. at Gauhati calling him 'Sir.' They suited him, and the extra rank probably got him the jeep that he was lent for his stay in Shillong. So we were lucky to be able to get around with picnics and see the very pretty countryside. It was about 5,000 feet up, and the climate warm but not too hot – rather like a good English Summer. The town itself had been built by the British as an H.Q. for Assam. There was a Government House and an air of suburban England.

One day we saw some Naga tribesmen dressed in their colourful finery and carrying spears, and were told that they were there for the wedding of their Queen.*

The tale we heard then, at Shillong, was that for years the Nagas had a legend that one day a great white Queen would come from overseas. So when a party of archeologists, including a tall young English woman, came touring round the Naga hills, the tribesmen saw this young woman and they asked her to come and be their Queen. At first she refused gracefully, but when the Japs invaded Burma, the British authorities asked her to take up this offer. She was made a member of Intelligence, with the rank of Colonel, and did great work for her country keeping the Nagas loyal to the British. There were tales of parties of our troops who were led through the jungle to safety by Naga guides. Others who came back with messages reporting movements of the Japs. Nagas could always be trusted, even when things looked bad for the British. ·

They protected their Queen with an armed Guard of honour, even when she went to Calcutta. There was a story that when she went dancing at the '400' Club, she left her Guard outside telling them that she would be out by a certain time. But she enjoyed herself dancing and didn't come out – so the Naga Guards went in to rescue her! She was now marrying a British Colonel, and the wedding was in Shillong.

One day we took a picnic and drove to Chera Punji. This was a village about forty miles away, on the other side of the Khasi hills. Here we were in another world – one that had 400 inches of rain a year, in fact the highest rainfall in the world. The day we went was one of the few days that it wasn't raining, but there was so much moisture in the air that one could almost see it. This was the place that the army chose as their H.Q. in the early days of British settlement – when just over the hills was Shillong with its almost perfect climate.

A guide took us round, and showed us the remains of the little stone built huts that our troops had lived in with no comforts of civilisation, and just day after day of rain. We saw the many waterfalls, and the precipice over which many of our men had thrown themselves, when they could stand the life no longer. We

* Ursula Graham-Bower, Author of "NAGA PATH", John Murray.

went into the caves and little boys showed us around, carrying Bamboo torches to light the way. The place still seemed to give off an air of misery and the hopelessness that our troops must have suffered there.

Bob took me to several dances, either at the Club or at Messes around, and how lovely it was to wear evening dresses again. On one of his last evenings, we walked outside and I tripped on a stone step and came down on my knee with an awful whack. I got absolutely no sympathy from the rest of the party, as they all thought it was an excuse to go off on our own.

For we were engaged to be married and both very happy. Fate had kept throwing us together. First by my getting ill and staying behind, and then Bob's Movement order arriving in the nick of time to take me up to Shillong: coincidences almost as strange as those of Verity and Peter's two meetings. Now, though, he had to report to Calcutta to travel on. There he chose me an Engagement ring and sent it to me at Shillong. Its emerald and diamond setting I thought, wwas, prettiest I had ever seen.

Before leaving, Bob had taken me to the British hospital where the Doctor said that I had water on the knee. I wasn't able to walk much and accused Bob of pushing me down on purpose so that I wouldn't be able to get around after he left. In a way it was lucky, as I really got a chance to rest and strengthen up, and I had the companionship of the very nice Sister who was hobbling around as well.

Also another V.A.D. was on leave from Sylhet. I had first met her when she arrived at the Cambridge hospital in 1943, so we had much to talk about – what a change in our lives since those Aldershot days! Her present hospital was much larger than our Panitola one, and had the added complication of taking West African patients. Both for racial and religious grounds they and the Indians had to be nursed in separate wards, and so made a third division to be catered for.

She had had a varied and interesting War, and was probably one of the most experienced of us V.A.D.s in India. During the evacuation of Dunkirk she was at Shornecliffe: from there she went to a C.C.S., with much of the time on eight hour shifts dealing with casualties from the Battle of Britain; and finally she got a posting to the Cambridge.

Here she had another sort of training with all the routine and discipline of a first rate hospital. What's more, Matron put her on Ward seven, under one of the most notoriously efficient Sisters – known affectionately as 'Tessie the Tank.' Tessie ran that ward with a rod of iron. There were no antibiotics in those days, so cleanliness and tidiness were essential, and the outer manifestation of perfection of treatment. There were mostly abdominal cases, who for the first few days after operations would have the utmost care and attention, and all were treated as bed-patients until their stitches were taken out. So it would be over a week before a hernia was allowed up and, as he got better, he had to fall in with ward rules. Beds were made in the morning with great neatness, and no patient must move in them until Matron had done her Round.

I well remember Tessie's clarion call. "Nurse, that bed is untidy. Go and see to it."

I scurried down the ward and carefully retucked the sheets. "Don't dare to move again until Matron has been," I hissed at the poor man.

"The discipline here is worse than anything that we have in the Guards," he grumbled back.

But I don't remember patients ever getting infections after operations. No germs could have existed on that ward. I don't think any patients ever died – they wouldn't have dared to!

It was fun talking over old memories with her, and I had a happy peaceful end to my three weeks.

When I went in front of the Hospital Board to be passed fit to return, I found that the O.C. taking it was the kind colonel who had met us ten V.A.D.s at Gauhati on our way up to Panitola. On the strength of my knee, he offered me an extra week's Leave. I thanked him but refused it, saying that I might miss my hospital, which was in transit at Chittagong.

On enquiry, I heard that an Ambulance train had arrived at Sylhet with patients for the Shillong hospital, and would be returning next afternoon for Chittagong. If I could catch that my journey would be a lot easier.

There was no army transport going down but I booked a first

class seat on the civilian bus due to arrive at Sylhet by lunchtime, and the hospital would warn the R.T.O. of my joining the train.

Next day I boarded the rather ramshackle little bus, and found that First Class meant the front seat by the driver. I was the only Britisher, and my fellow passengers mainly Indian families returning from holidays in Shillong.

The road was narrow and wound in and out around the hills as it gradually descended to the plain below. There being no room for cars to pass, there was a Time Schedule. So many hours for traffic going down, and then the following same number of hours for traffic coming up. In places there were deep gorges on the side of the road and the scenery quite breathtaking. My seat certainly gave me a first class view, but at times it felt quite terrifying.

The Driver kept going at a good speed as we went down but, once past the time barrier, he slowed. The passengers behind wanted to buy some of the many goods on display at the side of the road, and he obligingly stopped and joined in the noisy bargaining that went on. I got worried about the delay but time meant nothing to the Driver and the other passengers. Eventually we restarted, complete with several baskets of fruit and several live chickens.

At last we pulled up at Sylhet station, where we were met by a very worried Indian R.T.O. He had been told that I was on the bus and, with difficulty, was holding the train for me. With abuse at the Bus driver for being late, and a stream of orders, he had my luggage out and, almost running, he led us to a siding where the train was about to pull out. More shouts and commands, and finally I was helped up on to the train and my luggage thrown in after me. A minute later the whistle went and we were off.

It all reminded me of the frantic rush of our departure from Calcutta the year before, but now how different this train was. It was empty, except for an Indian Doctor and the British Nursing Orderlies, so I was given the Sisters' compartment with a private bathroom and proper bath. I was only on the train for one night but I had three baths, for I guessed that they might be my last for a long time – besides which it was again very, very hot.

Meals were laid on and the orderlies brought me cups of tea

and also an invitation from the M.O. to have dinner with him that evening.

On arrival at the Dining saloon, I was greeted politely by the young Indian doctor, and we sat down to a four course meal and drinks to go with it, and really good restaurant service. "My," I thought. "What a really cushy job this chap has got!" Unfortunately he drank more than was good for him and, seeing the disapproval in my eye, he started running down the British and anything to do with us. I suggested that after the War we might be glad to leave and give India her freedom.

At that he got really angry, and told me that I didn't know what I was talking about. "You British will never leave India. You make too much money from us."

It was the first time that I had heard an Indian talk like that. We had been lucky with our British doctors, who were mostly middle-aged and all polite and kind to us, and the Indian doctors had followed their example.

I got up saying a firm 'Good night' and, on opening the door, was surprised to find the orderly sergeant sitting on a chair outside. He gave me a fatherly smile of approval and said that he was was waiting to escort me back to my compartment. At this, I realised that my host probably had quite a reputation, and may have given trouble to sisters in the past.

On arrival at Chittagong, I was still wearing my khaki shirt and slacks. Usually in khaki we wore nothing on our heads but, as it was easier to wear than to pack, I had on my navy-blue peaked cap, which later I found was just as well. I got a lift to the hospital and reported to the Matron of 68 I.G.H., only to find that the staff of 49. had left just the day before, on a troop-ship for Rangoon.

It was too sickening, especially when I remembered the extra week's leave that I'd turned down. Quite shattering too when Matron said that I wouldn't be on 49's strength any longer. I exclaimed in horror, so then she did look me up and found that there were instructions for me to follow on as soon as possible.

"In the meantime," said Matron, "You can work here." Home Sister showed me into a really dirty Basha room that smelt like a latrine. The thunderbox in the bathroom was encrusted with dirt, and I wondered what sort of a hospital I had come to.

I found that I was the only V.A.D. in the block and the others were all Q.A.s waiting in transit for Rangoon too.

My neighbour was a young sister called Joan, who was on her way to a Casualty Clearing Station in Burma. She explained things to me. "Matron makes a very good thing out of us all and slaps us on duty and gets every ounce of work out of us that she can. They don't know what real work is here, and all they go in for is spit and polish, and I do just as little of it as I can get away with. By the way," she added, "it was lucky that you were wearing a cap when you arrived for we must never be seen in uniform without something on our heads. So this evening tie your hair up in a khaki head scarf." She was only young, but had been out long enough to get thoroughly bolshie about rank and seniority, and was a delightful neighbour to have next door.

The rest of the hospital and the Mess was a very different place: a peace time hospital, with the rules and discipline that went with it. It was spotless and well-run with the aid of us transit nurses. I was put on duty on the Major Surgical ward right next door to Matron's office, so that we had to look busy all the time which was difficult, as there was a large staff and few patients.

Just behind the ward was the Sisters' lavatory. A very smart one with running water and pull plug. My second day on duty I saw a typed notice had been put up there. "O.C. Sisters' lavatory – Nurse Robertson." I thought that it must be a joke, but my Ward Sister said not, and that Matron always liked one of us to be in charge of it. I asked what on earth I had to do?

"Don't worry," she said, "you only have to see that the sweeper cleans it. Then each morning, before Matron's round, go in with the Flit gun and spray around so it all smells nice and the seat looks polished. Matron is very particular about it looking polished."

This I successfully did each morning. All very hygienic, but I just wished she would have a look at our thunderboxes instead. Unfortunately, none of us transit girls had the courage to complain. However, if anyone in later years should ask me what I did in the war, I could say that, "I was O.C. Sisters' lavatory."

After a week, I was promoted to a Minor Surgical ward upstairs where there was one sister, two orderlies, and myself. We were either very busy or had little to do. One morning early, fifty patients had been evacuated on to an ambulance train. When we came on at 8 a.m. it was to find everything in a shambles, chaos everywhere, and the colonel's weekly inspection at 10 a.m. I felt quite faint at the sight. We each took an orderly to help and made beds as fast as we could go, and in that heat bed-making was no joke. No blankets, but still fifty mattresses to turn, then a rubber sheet, two sheets and a counterpane on each bed. By 10 a.m. the ward was tidy, the beds having been neatly lined up with a string, and we were standing to attention, dripping with heat when the colonel came round. I think that for the rest of the day, we just sat down and got over it.

I had been to the Registrar in the hopes of moving on. He said that I was lucky to have missed going with the others as their luggage had gone a day ahead in a separate ship, and had been left out in the monsoon rain until they arrived. 49. hadn't started functioning as a unit yet and the staff were helping at another hospital. "So you might just as well be helping here, as there," he said. "Don't worry, a boat may come in any day, and there are four sisters for it as well."

So I made the most of my off-duty and there were plenty of dances and beach parties. One half-day a party of us drove to the beach and bathed. The water was warm and I stayed in for an hour. The drive home too, was glorious, with the sun setting over the river.

It was six weeks since I had had any mail, as all my letters would have gone to 49. I found it difficult to write them myself – rather like writing to a brick wall with never an answer back. I wrote to Bob every day and just hoped that he would be getting my letters by now at Rangoon. A waste of time, as they didn't arrive until long after me.

At last at the end of a fortnight, I was told to be ready to sail next morning. Nine sisters and I set off complete with all our luggage and were taken out on a tender to a small Polish boat, that was filling rapidly with troops.

I shared a luxurious double cabin with Joan. At least it would have been luxury in the Baltic as it was fitted with central heating, but, alas, there were no fans. Joan looked at the other Q.A.s, who were all more, much more, senior and said, "If the Sick Bay ask for extra help, I bet that lot there will tell us two to go. So remember, we both get too seasick to be of any use."

We needn't have worried, as though the sea wasn't rough, we were seasick anyway since there was much vibration from the engines. Also, the monsoon rain poured down so there was no going on deck for fresh air.

One of our fellow passengers was an R.A.M.C. officer, also on his way to a hospital in Rangoon, and soon became "Doc" to one and all. As well as being a clever doctor, he was an amusing and altogether nice man, and quickly became the leading spirit of our medical crowd. He summed up us nursing staff, and took Joan and I under his wing – and it was astonishing how soon we got over being seasick once we had his company. He had the knack of getting a party going, and he made a good friend and companion to us.

One day the news broadcast said that there had been a new bomb dropped on a town in Japan, Hiroshima we thought it said. When the size of it was given, officers around gasped in astonishment. "That can't be right," one said. "This boat is Polish, so perhaps the radio crew are too, and have made a mistake." After that we forgot about it.

We were all glad when, after five nights, we anchored in the river by Rangoon. We girls were to wait on board until the last tender, so I spent the day leaning over the rails and watching the different units disembark. It was fascinating to see how different they were in their turnout and discipline. A company of Gurkhas were quickly away, all very smart and soldierly, each man with just a kitbag over his shoulder, whereas some of the other units seemed to be carrying everything but the kitchen sink, and shambled along with much noise and agitation. We guessed that they were probably our own Indian Medical Corps. We certainly were no example, as we had a mass of luggage between us.

Whoever planned the disembarkation hadn't allowed for that, as we certainly couldn't manage our tin boxes and bedding rolls and camp kit. So the ship's crew had to get us off and on to the tender. When we got to the dockside, who should be waiting but Bob, and it was a great reunion. He had heard that there was a troopship coming in that day and came down on spec. to see if I was on it. He spoke to one of the first British officers coming off, and asked if there were any V.A.Ds on board.

"Why do you want to know," the man asked suspiciously. Bob explained and gave my name. At which he became friendly and said, "Oh, yes. She is there."

"I suppose you are an old patient of hers?" said Bob.

"Why, yes, I was. How did you guess?"

When Bob realised about our luggage predicament, he rounded up some labour, and he himself helped load the boxes on to the two waiting lorries. When all was aboard, he expected to give me a lift in his jeep to the Y.W.C.A. To his annoyance, Senior Sister, who was also going to 49. refused to allow it, saying that I must go with them. He never forgave her for that, making a big story of it: how he had waited six hours in the sun, lumped all our luggage for us, and then wasn't trusted to drive me.

On arrival at the Y.W., Miss Sherbourne gave me such a very warm welcome. It was two months since they had left me at Dibrugarh, and it was really nice to see her friendly face again. She said that the hospital was to open in Rangoon's old Law Courts. But they had been left in the most awful state, and there was still much work to be done before 49. could open up for patients. She was slowly collecting a staff of sisters and they were working daily, cleaning, and settling in ward by ward, but it would be another month before it would be fit to be opened. In the meantime, our V.A.D.s had been attached to 38 B.G.H. who were in a pre-war hospital building.

"However," she said, "I expect you'd like a few days to get used to things, and I've got a whole pile of mail for you."

The Japs had left Rangoon very dilapidated with no electricity or running water but our Engineers had been working hard getting things partly going. The Y.W. had running water, but no electricity and, of course, no fans. The lavatories were pull plugs but Eastern ones, which meant no seat but a hole in the floor: very handy for Eastern ladies in their long skirts, but definitely tricky for us wearing slacks and trying to balance a torch at the same time.

The English women running the place did wonders with the

rations and I was able to have Bob in to dinner and to hear his news. He had arrived at Rangoon only to find that the unit had given him up as having gone on leave, and had promoted one of their own men. Fortunately, his Movement Order was from G.H.Q., and he was able to show that it was written on 7th May, though his own H.Q. didn't get it until 24th June, by which time he had already been replaced. Calcutta however, hadn't known this when he had reported there, and so still sent him on. Now here he was still waiting around for a fresh movement order, and worrying that he might be gone before I arrived. Communications were so bad over long distances, and so much time was wasted hanging around – as we V.A.D.s had already found.

When 49. had arrived in Rangoon, Bob went looking for me there and so met Matron. I think that it was partly for his sake that she allowed me the extra days off-duty, for Miss Sherbourne took a caring interest in her staff off-duty as well as on. I noticed her watching us, and summing him up and liking what she saw.

Bob was billeted at a Mess whose C.O. was Colonel 'Jock' Macdonald, and he took me there to dinner to meet him. I was interested to find that he came from the Isle of Skye in Scotland, and so told him how I was a descendent of Flora Macdonald, the Scottish heroine. This resulted in him saying later on, "Good night" as he shook my hand. "If ever you are in need of transport all you have to do is to ring me up, and I will send some round."

This was a wonderful offer and one that I was glad to take up later. In the meantime he lent Bob a jeep in which we were able to get around. In spite of being rather dilapidated after three years' occupation by the Japs, Rangoon looked surprisingly clean compared with Calcutta and, before the war, it must have been a beautiful city. Being built on the river estuary it was easy both to drive out to Monkey Point and get the sea breezes, or inland to where there was open country around the lakes. Half the population had evacuated when the Japs had originally bombed, and then taken, Rangoon. So the streets looked empty and were both wide and straight. Little of the bomb damage had been repaired, so pot-holes were everywhere.

The city is dominated by the Shay Dagon Pagoda which is truly one of the wonders of the world, with a great golden dome surmounted by a tall tapering pinnacle stretching up into the sky. The Pagoda had been built as a shrine for some of the hairs from the Buddha's head, long, long ago, in the days of the civilisation that had flourished in Burma while Britain was still in the Dark Ages.

The Shay Dagon's breathtaking beauty could be seen for miles around, as it towered over the town and surrounding plain. Driving round the city, one would turn a corner and there, suddenly, would be the golden outline standing out in sharp contrast to the modern buildings below, reminding us that it had stood there for centuries while nations and conquerors came and went, and would still be there long after we British would all have left.

One morning Bob and I went to see the temples and shrines around the base of it. We took off our shoes at the entrance and because the marble floor was so very, very dirty, I had taken the precaution of wearing two pairs of socks. It was wonderful that the temple had given refuge to so many people during the occupation but, on close view, the gorgeous, bejewelled statues and shrines looked in need of a really good wash.

The old British Swimming club was open, but only once a week for ladies. As usual the enterprising Chinese had opened a restaurant in the town. There was also a basha restaurant on the shores of a lake outside Rangoon called 'The Marina', after the Duchess of Kent. In some ways time had stood still. For instance we saw a stall of English books on the pavement, but they were all pre-war and so very out of date. The poor owner of the stall looked sad when we didn't buy anything, as he must have so carefully hidden those books away from the Japs.

Government House, a vast impressive building, was open as an Officer's club, and we went there to dance in its huge ballroom. I noticed a blonde Women's Army Service Burma – shortened in speech to WAS. B. – who was dancing with a British naval officer. The last time I had seen her was at Shillong, and there she had been wearing a long white evening dress, sculpted to her figure. With her platinum blonde hair and chiselled features, she looked startlingly beautiful as she danced cheek to cheek with her American escort. I asked about her, and was told that she was a

WAS. B. whose husband was fighting in Burma.

Now here in Burma she wore her uniform but still managed to look seductive in spite of her khaki shirt and slacks. Again I wondered where her husband was?

On 14th August we had dinner and went out for a walk. It was then that we heard the first sounds of cheering in the distance, and that was the first we knew of the Japs' surrender. We heard the news afterwards on the radio of the Y.W., but it was so sudden it was difficult to comprehend. For the Japanese never surrendered. They fought on until they were killed, or they committed suicide. That was why the fighting was so very bitter all the long way down through Burma. They would never have surrendered until Japan itself was taken, and there were thousands, or millions more casualties. What had happened?

Not until the next day when a brigadier came to the Y.W. himself, to give us the news, did it really sink in. He said there was to be a Victory Ball at Government House, and he invited us all to go, and told us to forget anti-malaria rules, and to wear our prettiest evening dresses.

That night Rangoon went mad. Bob and I were at the Ball but took refuge on a balcony overlooking the ballroom, and watched the amazing scene down below. There were hundreds and hundreds of uproariously happy officers charging around the floor in Rugger scrums. At one time some officers from a Tank regiment tried to drive a Sherman tank up the steps and into Government House. The M.P.s had to make a cordon across to stop them charging through the doors at the top. Everyone was mad with excitement and cheering wildly – at last the war was over.

12

My few days were up and I moved to 38 B.G.H., an all British hospital, with Indian servants for the cleaning only. It was good to join the other V.A.D.s – so much had happened to all of us. Dorothy had married Harry, and now he was left behind in Assam hoping his demob. would come soon. Diane and Nancy had stayed behind in Base Hospitals. Now there were only five of us left from the original ten, though Lillian had joined, as a replacement, at Chittagong. Among my mail was a letter from Verity in which she said she was quietly waiting the arrival of her baby, due at the end of September. How thankful she must have been that the war was over. Peter had been in the thick of the fighting, and she had little news of him. Still, no news was always good news.

We V.A.D.s were in two downstairs rooms of separate bungalows. The Resident Sisters had rather naturally taken the best rooms with bathrooms upstairs. I was sharing a room with Myra and Jean. This just meant pulling out my campbed and tying the mosquito net to the wires overhead. We had no furniture, and lived out of our boxes. Being a British hospital, there were no bearers, but just a sweeper to do the floors. The Sisters all had ayahs, and Dorothy, Freda and Lillian had engaged one for themselves. We had no electric light in our bungalows but cold water ran for an hour each morning and afternoon. This made washing a rather chancy affair, depending on one's off duty. Here we were in European houses, with actually less comfort than we had had with our camp equipment in bamboo Bashas! But there was one big advantage – a good laundry and clean dresses every other day.

I started work on a British Surgical ward. In the hospital there was water and electric light, but no electric power so no fans and all boiling and sterilising had to be done on primus stoves. The rain had stopped, and it was very, very, very hot. Most people suffered from prickly heat and because of this, the colonel gave out an order that all male ranks were to go round stripped to the waist during the day. This shirtless state caused some confusion for us transit nurses, as we didn't know who were doctors and who were orderlies. I was dishing out lunch in the kitchen and handing plates for the orderlies to take into the ward, and tried to thrust a plate at a figure standing by me. He wouldn't take it and someone hissed, "It's the Colonel, Nurse."

Soon after my return, Myra and Jean were ordered to move on to a Casualty Clearing Station at Moulmein. Fighting was still going on, as the Japs in Burma either wouldn't give in, or hadn't heard of the surrender. This came as a shock and the others went over to see Matron. She was genuinely sad too, as the others had done the long six week journey from Dibrugarh with her and we V.A.D.s were now her only original nursing staff. She had refused to allow any more of us to go and she had probably picked the right girls as they were both adventurous, but it was sad for us to be split up – and now we were only three.

Matron said that we might be back with her sooner than expected, as thousands of British P.O.W.s were coming very soon. Work was being rushed ahead in the hospital and the sisters were hard at work getting it cleaned up. We V.A.D.s took an unkind pleasure in the thought of the Sisters doing the cleaning, and joked among ourselves hoping that they were doing it thoroughly.

Bob, by now, had a new Movement Order back up to Imphal in Northern Assam. He left on 19th August. This time he was to do the journey partly by air and the rest by boat up the Chindwin. His first letter arrived after the air-flight, and he was staying at the local Pioneer Mess. Funnily enough, they had only just heard of the end of the war and had a March Past and two days' holiday. "My old company are near here and coming in by ones and twos since my arrival, to pay their respects."

This was the Pioneer Company that he had worked with during the siege of Imphal and he had since been awarded a Mention in Dispatches. His Pioneers had been armed for this battle, and he modestly said that he was more in danger from them, than from the Japs. The men had never before had training with arms and were as likely to shoot each other as the enemy. Bob warned me that the next stage of the journey would take eight days upstream so it would be some time before I would get another letter.

I was now able to answer the pile of mail that I had found at Rangoon. Because of censorship, we had never been able to give addresses or names of places. Just C.M.H. Panitola, S.E.A.C. Neither did we mention the names of any units or divisions either. This made a sort of guessing game for my parents, and when they heard that I was attached to 49. I.G.H. (c), they jumped to the conclusion that I was on my way to China – perhaps because I wrote of going by troopship. So I had to write, "No, we are not going to China, nor are we anything to do with the Chinese. (c) means Combined British and Indian troops." Now with the War over, at least I could say that we were in Rangoon.

After Myra and Jean left for Moulmein, I had our room to myself in peace and privacy but, that same night, the other three V.A.D.s had a nasty fright. Lilian woke up to find a man leaning over her bed, and holding her down with his hands on her shoulders. She yelled out, and Freda, who was a large upstanding girl, leapt from her bed to attack him. He took fright and ran, with Freda chasing after him right down the length of the verandah. He got away but she identified him as a British soldier.

It was a brave act chasing this would-be Rapist, but no one was surprised. For Freda was now a very different girl to the one last year in Calcutta, who had run into our room shrieking that there was a rat in the passage. She had matured and changed – as had we all. For we had been stretched to the utmost by our work, and learned to act and depend on ourselves. It wasn't just the thousands of miles we had travelled that separated us from home. It was that year of incredible responsibilities and, at times, the difficulties that we had to cope with on our own. Nothing now surprised us. We took things as they came and as best we could. Now if Freda should again meet a rat in the Grand Hotel, the rat would certainly come off the worse for the encounter.

When Matron heard, she said that they must move from that bungalow and join me in my room, so that we four would be together. It had never occurred to any of us to be nervous before this. At Panitola we had a barbed wire surround and guards, but everywhere else our rooms had been open. Now I was glad of the company of the others, but also delighted to share the help of the capable ayah whom the other three employed.

In the hospital I was on Officers' ward, but there were very few patients. One of them was a major, blinded in action. One eye had gone but there was still hope for the other. Every few hours this eye had to be washed out, drops put in, and then a fresh dressing. Sister explained this to me on my first day, and that he was to be flown home for an operation. She said that his WAS. B wife would be going with him. "She is an absolute Bitch," she added, "and I don't think wants go to."

My first afternoon on duty she came to visit him and I recognised her as the girl I had seen dancing at Government House. Outside, on the verandah, waited her naval friend. She looked and spoke in a very bored way, and mostly just sat in silence beside her blind husband. Her husband was a truly wonderful man, never complaining, and had the admiration and affection of all the nursing staff as well as his fellow patients, much sympathy too, that she should have her boy–friend sitting so blatantly outside.

One day in the office while taking the report from Sister, I said something waspish about her. The young M.O. was there and he fairly ticked me off. "Nurse, you must have more compassion," he said. "That poor girl married a Regular Army Officer, and she is not cut out for the new life she has to face."

Sister and I looked at each other, "What fools men are," we signalled with our eyes. For this doctor too, was under her spell and spent much time talking to her. But perhaps he was right.

"She wants to help and doesn't know how," he said. "Let her watch you when you next wash his eye out."

So that evening when I brought the dressing tray, I asked her to stay and help me. "Oh no, Nurse, really I can't," she said in a tone of revulsion. Then later, and again in front of her husband: "Nurse, would you like to take my place in the 'plane and go to England with my husband? You would be much more help to him," she urged.

"No I'm sorry that's not possible," I answered, and for his sake tried to keep the ice out of my voice.

Many years later and quite by chance, I heard again of this major, and how his marriage had, rather naturally, broken up. My informant was full of praise for him, and of the success he was making of his new life.

The hospital was being rapidly evacuated to get ready for the expected rush of prisoners of war released from Jap camps, and there was less and less to do on the wards. One day I saved myself a treat from the patients' lunch – some tinned pineapple – and was busy eating it in the office, when who should walk in but 'Doc,' from boardship. I was pleased to see him but would have liked him to find me doing something useful. But oh no! There I was, sitting down, guzzling the patients' rations.

"So this is where you are," said Doc, taking in the scene at a glance and also my discomforture. "Well Nurse, I see that I'm too late for any pineapple but perhaps you can still spare me a cup of tea," and he sat down grinning hugely.

When there is little to do, Army hospitals have a way of shaking everyone up by moving. Matron couldn't do that, but she did the next best thing and swapped all the wards round in a general post.

It was an incredible day. Sister was going on night-duty that evening so was on duty till 1 p.m., and I was off between ten and one and then on until 8 p.m. I arrived to find our ward moving to another block and up two flights of stairs – 56 steps in all. Orderlies were carrying our stuff out, while the other wards were bringing theirs in.

My Sister had warned me that the incoming one was a real terror and not to be trusted, a she was liable 'to make' items of our equipment for her ward. 'Making' actually means stealing army property but, when it was for the ward, it was sometimes practised by the most surprising people. In England I remembered a sister, Plymouth Brethren by denomination, who had to be watched in and out of any ward that she visited.

Well, I checked and rechecked every item and stacked it all away upstairs without this new sister getting near it. I was supposed to stay behind in the old ward, not being part of the equipment, but was so alarmed by her manner and reputation that I decided to remove myself as well. Later I heard that the Terror had accused my new sister of having stolen both her primus stove and her nurse – in that order.

By 5 p.m. we had got our remaining two patients settled into the new ward, all safe and secure, as I thought. The sister and orderlies went off duty and left me in sole possession, until a very worried looking young M.O. came in. This was his ward, and he had just signed for all the equipment and then found that there were no bedpans or bottles in the latrine. "I daren't ask that sister for them. She would never let them go."

I suggested that we slip into my old ward by a side entrance when she wasn't around and then help ourselves. This we successfully did, and were crossing back over the central court-yard with our arms piled high with bedpans and bottles, when we walked straight into the Terror and the Colonel.

"Nurse, where did you get those?" she demanded furiously. I turned to my companion for help but he looked too petrified for speech. The Colonel was meanwhile shaking with laughter, but came forward to my rescue.

"It's all right, Sister. Leave this to me," he said. "I'll deal with it later." We thankfully escaped and put our rescued treasures away.

Everything was being got ready for the arrival of the British P.O.W.s from Bangkok. One afternoon, a Psychiatrist came and gave a lecture for all sisters and nurses to attend. Lady Louis Mountbatten and a Red Cross team had flown into Bangkok to visit some of the camps. They saw and heard of the appalling conditions that our men had been living and working in during the last three and a half years. The officers had been put into separate camps so that the men would be leaderless, otherwise they were all treated the same. This meant unbelievably badly, and they had been working as slave labour on the Bangkok to Moulmein 'Death Railway.' Japs didn't believe in surrender so no humiliation was too bad for our men. They had subsisted on little but boiled rice, and then only when fit to work.

We had to expect the morale of these coming prisoners to be especially low. They had been cut off from all news of the outside world, and few of them had heard from their families. We would be the first white women that they would have seen for years, and our reaction to them could make all the difference to how they reacted to women back home. They would need to talk, and we must listen. He told us details of their suffering, and the various effects it might have on them. The main thing was that we must watch our step, as our behaviour could effect their return to their families.

Though the war was over, the actual surrender arrangements were slow, and it was two weeks before the first P.O.W.s, or R.A.P.W.I., pronounced RAP. WI., arrived. In the meantime we carried on with just a few patients in each ward.

Bob had left on his long journey back up to north Burma and I still hadn't heard from him, and the days and evenings went by very slowly. To cheer me up, Doc invited me as his guest to the Ladies'·night party that his Mess was giving, and I looked forward to it.

I got on well with my new Ward Sister until two Transit Q.A.s were added to our ward. They were a different type altogether and like my friend Joan, at Chittagong, had no intention of exerting themselves while with us. Sister gave up trying to give them orders and she and I did the work between us.

Not that there was much to do with only a few patients, but the heat and humidity were fearful and difficult to stand. Those fifty six steps felt more like a hundred and fifty six, and my quick way of walking round the wards soon turned into a languid stroll. How it annoyed me to see those two lazy sisters sitting in a sideward and gossiping all morning, while my gentle Ward Sister would say nothing. Aggravating too, that our ward was the only one in the hospital to have an early breakfast at seven thirty. This meant that a sister had to be there to dish out the breakfasts, and Sister and I shared this duty on alternate mornings, for she never dared to tell the other two to take their turn. Gradually tempers became frayed and, in my case, ended in a stupid and uncharacteristic rebellion which caused a small furore in the hospital.

The day came when we all four in our room came off duty at five and found that the ayah had forgotten to fill the bath, during the one hour of running water. At least she had filled the small, very small, canvas buckets so we could have a wash, but then there was the problem of the lavatory. By four next day it would be very smelly, unless we spared some of our precious bucket water to flush it out. Oh. How we longed for our old thunder-boxes, which we used so to deride.

Nor could we take turns to soak in the bath, and so cool off both our minds and our bodies. To top it all, it was my turn to be on duty for the early breakfast next morning. That evening I decided that I wouldn't go on duty, and so perhaps show up the laziness of those two Transit Sisters. After all, the two ward orderlies were quite capable of serving out the food for the four officer patients that we had in.

Next morning when I strolled in at 8 a.m. Sister asked me why I was so late.

"I thought that one of the new sisters would be doing breakfasts," said I, putting on an innocent expression. I expected her to tick me off and then I would tell her just what I thought about the other two.

For a moment she said nothing, and then: "Nurse, how could you," and she walked away leaving me feeling an absolute worm.

However Matron, when told, soon sorted both me and the situation out. Nurse Robertson to go on Night-duty to 'special' a seriously ill case was the solution, and also her punishment for me. Actually I didn't mind working on Nights as it would be cooler then, but I did mind missing the M.O.s party next evening.

When I told Doc and that he must find another partner, he was furious. "How damned stupid. I'll soon stop this."

"No, please don't do anything. I'm in enough trouble as it is," I pleaded.

At one o'clock I went off duty and to have a sleep ready for working through the night. Not for long as, to my astonishment, an orderly soon shook me awake. "Matron says that you are to go on Night-duty to-night. I'm sorry Nurse, but she told me to make sure that I told you personally," he explained to my indignant face.

I found later that Doc had written against the patient's name, "This man has improved and does not need 'specialing.' He should have known better and that it was enough to get any Matron's back up, but then I wasn't the only one to be feeling the heat. No wonder Matron had sent that orderly.

In the nick of time for me, that afternoon, the RAP. WI started arriving. The hospital became alive again and working as one unit, with past squabbles forgotten including my small crime. I was given two wards to look after, and had a really interesting Night-duty.

The RAP. WI were flown into Rangoon to be sorted out in the hospitals before going to Transit camps, and then on to England. These first arrivals were the fittest and some didn't stop more than a night or two, so each day there were new arrivals.

That evening, I walked slowly round the ward, greeting each man but not one would look up at me. The same thing happened in the second ward, but yet I felt conscious of all eyes being on me when I wasn't looking. I went round again with milk drinks, and still no response. I was beginning to feel nearly as shy as them and knew that I must make a break-through somehow. The Red Cross had sent old magazines and papers some of which lay on the centre table, so I went across and started looking at them. Gradually in twos and threes, the men came up and started asking questions. What was England like?

I found that they were too dazed to want to talk themselves. Everything was so shatteringly strange. Even being given a milk drink was overwhelming for some of them. What they did want to hear was about Britain and their home towns, and try to understand what had been going on. They were worried by the pictures of the V2 rocket bombs, and whether they had hurt their families.

It was later in a night or two, that they wanted to talk themselves, and, once talking they didn't stop. My horror and sympathy at their tales was so very genuine, however many times I should hear the same sort of ghastly story. Many of them found it difficult to sleep in their new surroundings and needed sedatives. Otherwise there was little to be done for them, as their only complaint was that the beds were too comfortable.

There was one noisy night when one of the men had brought in his pet monkey. It was shut in the bathroom and the poor thing made the most awful din. I wonder what happened to that monkey as the men must have been very fond of it.

During the big move, the blind major had been left in his old bed, so now he was among the RAP. WI. This turned out to be a great success as, because of his blindness, they weren't shy of him. He too, was interested in talking to them, and they got on well together. Many a time a P.O.W. said to me, "Do you know there is a wonderful chap upstairs who is quite blind, and we so like talking to him." One man added, "Do you know the Japs blinded him, but he says that he doesn't hate them."

As I had little to do for the rest of the night, I was given the job of three hourly penicillin injections at twelve, three and six o'clock, for about six of our ordinary patients. This sounds simple enough, but actually was a beastly job as the needles were so blunt, and each time that I boiled them, they became blunter.

The ships carrying our supplies had been diverted to Singapore and, with them, our new sharp needles. The laboratory technicians tried to sharpen the old ones, but they really were very blunt. So being punctured by them was a three hourly torture for the patients, and only when it was really necessary did the M.O. prescribe penicillin. They were all very ill men who felt that as soon as they had managed to get to sleep, I would wake them up again for another awful injection. Then each man took quite a bit of settling down with warm drinks etc, after which I reboiled the syringe and needles ready for the next painful session of jabs.

Working at night was much cooler and more pleasant, but sleeping by day was not easy, even though my bed had been moved out to a shady verandah. So I just dosed myself with the patients' sedatives and stopped thinking of the stories that they told me. Still, I had only five nights on duty as 49. opened up in a hurry, and Matron recalled us.

13

We'd got used to being independent and a boy-friend of Lilian's sent a couple of lorries, with strong men, to move us with all our baggage. 49's new Sisters' Mess was temporarily in two houses in a suburb of Rangoon and about three miles from the hospital. We arrived just in time for lunch, and Matron gave us a friendly greeting of, "Welcome home, Nurses," making it clear to everyone that we were some of her old staff.

The hospital was madly busy so we had to go on duty at five that evening. We four shared a downstairs room, and quickly got on with fixing up camp beds and mosquito nets. We now had a chair and locker each but no other furniture, so there was little unpacking to be done. Anyway things were so short in Rangoon that anything left out was liable to get stolen, and we spent much of our time locking and unlocking boxes, and wore the keys on strings round our necks.

Our room didn't have a bath, but we were to share one with some sisters in the next room. After unpacking we piled into their bathroom and revelled in cold baths and lovely clean water for each one of us. In this part of Rangoon there was running main water all the time which was a wonderful luxury at last. It must have been maddening for those sisters to have us taking over their bathroom like that, but they made the mistake of complaining to Matron that it was not right that they should have to share with V.A.D.s.

Matron sent for us four the next day and told us what they had said. "Now you mustn't take any notice of these new sisters," she advised. "The trouble is that they haven't been out here long enough to understand. However, I think that you would be happier if you shared the night-duty bathroom upstairs. It has a door on to the passage and, if you are quiet in the afternoons, you won't disturb them." So, in Miss Sherbourne's usual caring way, she settled us all down happily.

The first afternoon after bathing we changed into our khaki slacks and shirts, and then off to tea in the Mess which was in the other house. We went backwards and forwards to the hospital by army truck and, piling in with the others, we soon found that it was a good way to get to know each other – especially in the mornings when there was an awful scrum. We found that there were five new V.A.D.s from the second batch sent out that Spring, and also that most of the Q.A.s were from Base hospitals in India, nor had they been out very long.

A few days later however, I had a nice surprise, "Nurse," said the new Theatre Sister. "I'm told that you used to be at the Cambridge hospital in Aldershot. Do you remember me? My name is Cooper, and I was Theatre Sister there for some time."

I hadn't recognised her for, in those days I rarely saw her except in her theatre gown and mask. But I certainly did remember her, as she had been a by-word for discipline and efficiency in that very efficient hospital.

Sister Cooper, too, had been with the 14th Army for about a year and, though still keeping up her very high standards of work, off duty she treated us all as equals. By her example, she showed these new junior Q.A.s that, in Forward hospitals, all of us in the Sisters' Mess were equal companions in adversity. She had a happy face, and became a popular sister among us V.A.D.s. Perhaps not though, with some of the Q.A.s, on whom she was apt to use a special brand of dry humour.

The Burma Star ribbon had been awarded to those who had served in the 14th Army, and our Colonel now told all ranks to wear it. We sewed the ribbons on to little wire brooches, pinned on to whichever dress or shirt we were wearing. This gave us a certain status amongst the newcomers in the Mess.

In a letter home I said that there were some new V.A.D.s but I never mentioned them again, nor do I remember any of their names, or what they looked like. Perhaps they thought us unfriendly, but we never meant to be. It was just that we four had our own room, and somehow we felt a race apart from these new girls and had almost forgotten that we belonged to the Red Cross. Our allegiance was to 49 I.G.H. and to Miss Sherbourne, our

Matron, and we had become, quite literally, 'the Nurses'. I suppose all soldiers who have been in Battle feel rather different from others who have never seen any action. Those months of hard work, and heat, and sweat, somehow gave us a feeling of apartness. No wonder that when we first arrived at Panitola hospital, we had sensed this 'them' and 'us' situation. But now it was reversed, and it was we who looked on the newcomers with a slightly critical air.

We had good meals considering that after V.J. day most of our food supplies had been diverted to Singapore. The patients had full rations, but we were cut down to half. At an exorbitant price, Home Sister managed to buy some vegetables in the bazaar to supplement our food. Perhaps it was as well that it was so hot, so we hadn't much appetite anyway. We started both lunch and dinner with soup in which we added lots of salt. We dripped with heat so much that our systems craved extra salt, and the troops were issued with salt tablets. It was surprising how delicious any watery soup tasted with a teaspoon of salt added to it. Our second course was nearly always bully beef in some form or another. Water was heavily chlorinated at source, and so, tasted revolting. However, we were able to buy bottles of lime juice to disguise the taste. Meals out were always a treat.

The hospital was still being converted and workmen were everywhere. The old Law Courts was a vast building of three floors and big high-ceilinged rooms. Gradually ward after ward was being opened up and filled with P.O.W.s. They stayed with us for two or three days for tests, inoculations, dentist, oculist, etc. If all was well, they went off to a transit camp, otherwise their treatment started straight away. I was put on to what was to be eventually two Indian Surgical wards, though that evening they were filling up rapidly with P.O.W.s. The staff was Indian with nursing sepoys, none of whom spoke English. The place seemed chaotic, and I thought the Sister must be useless, until I realised that she was just as ignorant of Urdu, and the management of Indian staff, as I had been a year ago. She was grateful when I took charge of the ward staff to try and get them working. At first there was trouble, as they had been only too ready to let the patients do the work for them.

The P.O.W.s had been issued with khaki shorts at Bangkok, as all they had had from the Japs were loincloths. On arrival at the hospital, they queued up and the Quartermaster issued each one with a full set of clothes. They then came up to the wards and were shown a bed and a locker each. They were dazed and delighted with their new clothes, and really treasured them. There was no time for leisurely talking to patients. Just one mad rush to get them settled in by the evening, and all given a good meal.

We were two floors up. There was no running water and every drop had to be carried up by the pani-wallah and then, when used, carried down again. The food had to be fetched from the kitchen downstairs by the ward boys, and I would dish it out myself. Then the plates had to be washed up, and the dirty water carried down again.

The patients must have had wash rooms downstairs somewhere, as certainly not enough water could have been brought up for them. They loved washing, and spent much time washing their precious smalls, which they then hung on the mosquito nets to dry. The wards looked like dhobi lines, with clothes hanging round the beds.

All through the day the noise was horrendous. Workmen everywhere, and we could hardly hear ourselves speak with the hammering. The work was done by a unit of black African soldiers, and we were warned that there was friction between them and our Indian sepoys. To save trouble our Indian staff had a way of throwing used water out of the windows, instead of it being carried downstairs again. This caused rows, as it sometimes landed on the Africans below who thought it was done on purpose. I don't think it was actually aimed at them for, as I found out for myself later, one couldn't see who was down below.

There was electric light, but otherwise no modern amenities. All together, the noise and the seeming chaos must have been most matrons' idea of Hell. However, Miss Sherbourne took it all in her stride. She was a strong personality who didn't need to throw her weight about to show authority. She never seemed to get into a bad temper, and was kind to us all. I don't know how she kept so calm and serene. Most of us, including myself, found it difficult to keep our tempers at times in that very hot and humid atmosphere.

One day, I came on duty at 1 p.m. to be told by Sister that the sweeper had to go to the dentist again, so would I ask the patients to sweep the wards. This I knew happened the day before as well, and when I had expostulated about it to her, she just said, "Oh, the patients don't mind." I couldn't get her to understand that, in India, it was a great insult to be told to do sweeper's work, and that none of the other Indian staff would do it. After all these men had gone through, this seemed the final indignity.

When she had gone, I went along to the dentist, who had his surgery next door to our ward, and spotted our sweeper chatting away to a pal in a corner. He certainly wasn't queuing up for treatment. I went in and asked the Indian dentist to examine him quickly and explained the situation.

"Don't worry," he said, "I shall see to him." He certainly did see to him and pulled one of his teeth out.

Our sweeper arrived back very sorry for himself and clutching his jaw. I thought I had better uphold the dentist's summary justice, but gave him some aspirin. "This will help the pain. Now go and sweep both wards," I said hard-heartedly.

Later I inspected his work and sent him off duty. After this we had no more trouble with the ward staff, and certainly nobody asked us to be excused work for the dentist.

Our ward was settling down and we all worked well together. As Sister and I moved around among the patients, we listened to the awful stories the men had to tell of the Labour Camps that they had worked in on the Burma – or "Death" – Railway. It seemed incredible that any survived at all, least of all that their morale was still high. One man said that he could forgive the Japs anything except the way they left the sick to die. Their doctors and orderlies must have worked wonders with the little that they had to treat them with. One man came in with an artificial leg. Just a camp-made one, out of what the medical staff could lay their hands on. It weighed very heavily, but did the job all right.

Some of the camps sounded better than others – that is the men weren't knocked around so much – but most of them were appalling. The officers were in their own camps, but had to work just as hard, and were treated just as badly as their men.

On their arrival, we took details of the patients past illnesses. It seemed quite common for men to say that they had had malaria about thirty times, which meant that it was never out of their systems. Many of them had minor injuries, and skin ulcers, which all needed treatment. Dysentery and stomach upsets were common. They had had little but rice for years, and thought our Army rations wonderful.

The units around were doing their best to entertain the P.O.W.s and our patients were sometimes included. One evening, most of our two wards went to a party where they had such a good time that one man had to be left behind. His hosts gave him breakfast next morning and returned him distinctly the worse for wear. I revived him with A.P.C. medicine with such good effect that he came and asked me if I would go "walking out" with him. There was nothing wrong with his morale.

I 'phoned Colonel Macdonald and he, more than once, sent trucks to take patients to the Swimming Club for the afternoon. He even had the forethought to send an English speaking havildar with them.

Everyone rallied round to help, and it was a pleasure to us to join in when off duty. We were invited to a party that a Mess was giving for P.O.W. officers. They were too shy to ask us to dance, so the M.C. started a form of Paul Jones called "Snowball". He and three others asked four of us to dance, and when the music stopped, we all eight had to ask another eight to dance. I picked on a nice looking Lieut. who turned out to be a patient in our hospital. When the music stopped again, then all sixteen would look for new partners, so gradually the whole room was dancing and the ice broken. Tom, my first partner, came back to ask for a dance and he turned out to be a chatty and delightful partner.

Next morning he visited me on my ward and later came back to ask if I would go in a party of four to see a play being put on by ENSA – 'Normandy Story' with Winifred Shotter as the star. Of course I accepted, and found that the party was Eileen, our Welfare Officer for the P.O.W.s, and another patient. Eileen had laid on a staff car, and booked the best seats and we had a great evening.

Our two men were delighted with themselves, and had the enterprise to send a note to Winifred Shotter asking for an introduction. At the end of the show, she came to join us and was sweet to them. She flapped her enormous false eyelashes and chattered away about the play. She really made their evening, and we all returned in triumph to the hospital.

Tom Burns left for a transit camp and I soon had a letter posted from Colombo, saying that he was on a troopship for England. I am sure he must have made a success of the rest of his life. He had certainly come through the last three years with great courage.

In one of our wards, a patient sprang a temperature, and to everyone's surprise, the Medical Specialist diagnosed smallpox, which he must have picked up in Bangkok after release. He was hastily removed to an Isolation Hospital. The rest of the ward had to be vaccinated, and then all kept in with us for two weeks quarantine. None of their vaccinations took, but nobody else developed smallpox. At first they were disappointed at having their return home delayed, but they soon settled down happily. As I have said, they loved washing their smalls, but now they kept washing their shirts and trousers too. We had procured a flat iron for them, which they heated over an oil stove and a lot of their day was spent queueing up for the iron. They just wore a towel round their middles while they waited for their clothes to dry and be ironed.

Neither Sister nor I spoke of it to them, but why all this keenness to look clean and smart? Certainly not for us who were used to seeing them in only a towel. We both suspected that they were quietly slipping out of the hospital, in twos and threes to look around Rangoon. We neither of us blamed them, and they were very discreet over it. Sergeant Reid was their natural leader and he could have organised it very smoothly. We both knew that he would never let us know or get into trouble over it. So long as they were there for meals and the doctors' rounds, no one would notice a few absentees. Anyway, the washing and ironing kept them occupied.

They were a nice crowd and we soon got to know them all by name, and heard about their wives and families. One day I was just going off for lunch when their first batch of mail arrived, and the Sergeant was sorting it out. What excitement! They were all so thrilled. I could hardly wait, myself, to get back and hear their news. When I did return, it was to find a changed ward. The men just slouched about, or lay on their beds without speaking. I couldn't understand what had happened. Weren't they pleased to get their letters?

At last it came out. One of the men had heard from his wife that she wanted a divorce. Another wife wrote saying that she had a baby of a year old. The thoughtless cruelty of it. It seemed so unbelievably selfish. Why couldn't they have let their men come home first, for now all the others were wondering what reception they would get when they got home. It took a long time for them to get over it. They were lucky to have such a strong character as Sergeant Reid with them and it was partly to his credit that morale gradually rose again. So, if they were slipping out of the hospital, we didn't blame them.

Matron did her morning rounds, and sometimes sat on a bed and talked to the men, seemingly oblivious to the lines of washing around her. Towards the end of September, no more P.O.W.s were admitted to our hospital, and before long, our second ward was empty and there were only 250 in the whole hospital. The whisper went round that we were to close and move on again, perhaps to Saigon.

It was about three weeks before I heard from Bob again and then several letters came at once. He had had an uneventful voyage up-river and was very glad to get there. Many of his letters were written at night by light of the Burmese moon that made it almost as bright as day-light. He described the wonderful orchids that grew wild in the jungle, and how, now that the Japs had gone, the village girls decorated their hair with them, and how colourful they looked. He bought me a ruby, which later he had done up in a ring. And always his letters were full of how much he missed me.

He was thankful to arrive but not nearly so glad as his C.O. who had been waiting for his arrival before he himself could go on leave. So, Bob temporarily took over all units up there. Many of them were Tamils from Southern India and they and their officers were delighted to find that he spoke their language. He was able to smooth out several difficulties that had been caused by none of their British officers speaking Tamil.

I had been trying to write to him every day, but at times it was a great effort as with no electric light, it meant sitting close to a hurricane lamp to be able to see and then we got hotter than ever. He, too, was getting my letters in batches. Priority was given for mail to England – for the sake of the P.O.W.s – but Matron had made an arrangement to collect our letters and send them by priority as well. We gave them to her in the truck each morning, and Dorothy and I found she kept us up to the mark for our men's morale. "Nurse Robertson, no letters from you again. This won't do," she would tease. I told Bob how regularly I was trying to write and even Matron was on his side.

Bob had told me in his first letter to get out, and not sit around the Mess in the evenings. But when he heard about so many parties, he began to have his doubts, and the wretched George came in for much criticism. George had been a friend of Myra's, and all he ever wanted was some company out of his own Mess. So Dorothy and I were grateful to be squired around by him, generally in a threesome. Sometimes when it was very hot and our nerves on edge, he would drive us down to the river and we would just sit and cool off in the sea-breezes. We would watch the boats and the comings and goings, just quietly sitting without saying a word. Oh, the peace and quiet of those evenings, when we three watched the clanking and bustle of the ships being unloaded. The peace of that river, lapping against the dockside, and the wonderful quiet that healed our minds. On moonlight nights the moon shone so brilliantly, far brighter than anywhere in Europe, and extra lights were hardly needed for working by. As we three sat, each thinking our own thoughts, the War and its aftermath sank further away and, gradually, we would unwind and our nerves be restored for another day.

One evening, George took us in a party to the Marina restaurant, where a crowd of P.O.W. officers were being entertained as guests of a local Mess. After dinner, a young Australian WAS. BI. jumped up on a table and started singing in a clear strong voice. She sang well-known dance songs, and soon had the whole room joining in. Then she called out to us few girls to dance, while she beat out the time by the clapping of her hands. So we girls and our partners danced, while the others all sang as they, too, clapped out the beat. The P.O.W.s faces were alive with joy, and they looked so happy that we were all happy too. Then we sat down and everyone sang songs, and it was a lovely evening.

By now I had acquired a Military driving licence as a staff officer, going home on Repat. had handed them out to any of us girls who said she held an English licence. So I telephoned Colonel Macdonald and, one afternoon, he sent me his jeep to practice in. His driver took me and another girl out of Rangoon and on to the Pegu road, and there he stopped and got out. In a resigned voice he told us that the Colonel Sahib had said that I was to drive. There wasn't much traffic, and what there was slowly manoeuvred round the pot-holes, and I got in quite a bit of practice and so got the hang of it. After that, I drove anyones jeep who would let me, including that of George.

The Colonel sent me his jeep again and, with Sister's blessing, I filled up the back of it with patients from our ward that was not in isolation, and drove them round Rangoon to see the sights. We could never do anything without being noticed, and next day one of the doctors asked me, "Was that you I saw careering around Rangoon in a jeep endangering our patients' lives?" They have survived three and a half years with the Japs so it would be a pity if you killed them off now," and he went off laughing at his own wit.

At the end of September, the M.O.s gave a farewell party for Matron, who was going home to England on repat. We were all very sorry that she was leaving as we liked her so much. We were equally nervous of the new matron who was coming from a Base Hospital in Ceylon, but as usual, with the slowness of communications it was to be another month before she arrived. In the meantime, there was a nice, jolly Acting Matron.

Our P.O.W.s' two weeks quarantine was up, and they did a lovely thing for us. They all collected together in the morning and Sergeant Reid gave a speech. He thanked us for having them and giving them their first home for years. If he had gone on much longer, I think Sister and I would have been in tears. Then they gave us lovely presents which they had bought out of the little pocket money that they had been allowed. Sister had carved wooden book ends and, because Nurse was "going in for the Matrimonial Stakes," – cheers – they gave me a carved wooden tray, and ivory brooches for us both. They all signed their names on the tray and I treasure it, and the brooch, to this day.

They then left for the transit camp to embark on a troopship in a few days. "We shall write to you both from the ship and tell you all about it," they said. In the meantime, parties of them hitched over to see us each day, "Just to see how you're getting on." My parents had ordered a gift parcel of 500 cigarettes for my patients, which should have arrived months before. Suddenly they turned up in the nick of time, and I was able to give them as a present to these P.O.W.s.

14

Our ward was to turn back into an Indian Surgical. Workmen were still banging around in the hospital but, by now, it had become a background noise that we hardly noticed. Nevertheless, we did wonder why it was still going on, when all the talk was of the hospital closing down.

One day an officer called in to see me on the ward. At first I didn't recognise him and then I realised that it was Peter, Verity's husband. He had aged at least ten years in looks and was gaunt and sick looking – so different from the laughing young man who had waved goodbye last December. Thank God, though, that he was alive and whole. His unit had fought all the way down from Imphal and were now at Pegu waiting to go on to Bangkok. Verity's baby was due, but he had had no news for some time. I couldn't tell him anything either and could only say that all letters to India were very slow. I was so delighted to hear from her later that she had had a baby boy. I so hoped Peter would be able to get some leave to see her and have a rest. He certainly looked as though he needed it.

I didn't often go to ENSA shows but Gracie Fields and her Italian husband came to Rangoon. One afternoon, I went along to an open-air concert. It was hot and uncomfortable sitting on the ground and, to begin with, seemed dull. Why, oh why wasn't I having a nice rest on my bed with a book? Then Gracie came on and electrified the whole audience. She must have been hot and tired too, but she sang and sang, and we all knew why she was a STAR – and "Our Gracie".

Our wards filled up with troops: fighting troops mainly who, like Peter, had fought for months in Burma, some in a pitiful condition. I was glad to be busy and occupied, and the days weren't so hot. On 14th October, I woke cold at night and had to get a blanket. The hot weather was nearly over!

Bob wrote that on 20th September, he had been asked if he would accept 'B' release as his firm had applied for his return. He had filled in the necessary forms and was now waiting and waiting to hear when he would get it. At first he wrote to me that he would come down to Rangoon. Then he said for me to get leave to Calcutta and he would fly down. He seemed to think that I could leave at any time, but I had just as many forms to fill in and permissions to get. If I had been marrying someone returning to England, I would have been granted my release automatically, but there was nothing in our contract to allow us to marry and go to Ceylon. If I knew the Army, it would take months before it came through.

Dorothy had been through all this already, and been refused release. Now they were managing it with a wangle, as, though Harry was Indian Army, he had arranged to get his demob. in England. He would take four months leave there and then return to work in India so, going to England, she might go with him.

Our Registrar, Major Robertson, was my namesake. I certainly found that our Scottish Clans were helpful to each other. He wired HQ to make enquiries and eventually told me that I could apply for two weeks' leave to get married. He would then see that I got on to a boat plus all my luggage so that I needn't come back. "Things can be arranged," he said. The Acting Matron was equally kind and helpful.

I wrote to Vera Irwin in Calcutta and she straightaway replied for me to go there, and said they would give me my wedding from their house. She, herself, had met her husband while staying with my parents in Calcutta and they had given her her wedding. I had even been her bridesmaid at the age of three and she said that she had hauled me up the aisle at the end of her train.

As Bob's and my letters often took weeks to arrive, we kept writing to each other at cross purposes. Eventually, he said that he would get leave to Calcutta in the second week of November and would I apply for leave beforehand. That was all very well when no one knew when there would be a troopship, or even a berth on it. I began to feel sick with worry and, at times, wondered if I was doing the right thing. Then another really lovely letter would come from him, and I would feel happy again.

After Matron left, I decided to stop taking Mepacrine tablets. After all, I didn't want to be married with a jaundiced face and I just knew in my bones that I hadn't got malaria. Gradually, I became less yellow and I didn't develop malaria, and I felt rather pleased with myself.

On the wards, we still had to have all the water carried up and then down again. Now, with so many dressings to do, we kept needing to wash our hands. The pani-wallah hadn't yet learnt that he must bring up more water and, just as important, more empty buckets to tip the dirty water back into.

One morning, when Sister was going round with the surgeon, she called out to me to re-dress a patient's wound straightaway. I went to collect my dressing tray and scrub my hands and, of course, found a bowl of dirty water and no bucket to tip it into. There was a jug of clean water though, so I quickly slung the dirty water out of the window and refilled the basin with clean. I heard a yell from down below but thought no more of it. I quickly scrubbed up and dressed the man's leg.

When I returned, there was a black African sergeant waiting. He gave me a smart salute, and then said, "I am sorry, Sister, to have to report that one of your sepoys has just thrown dirty water over one of my men."

Oh dear! Just what we had been told mustn't happen, and I had done it myself. So, all I could say was, "Please tell your man that I am very sorry that it was I who threw the water. It was a mistake and I was in a great hurry."

He was so surprised that he just gave me another salute and went – and I heard no more. It was rather fun throwing that water, and I could well understand how our staff had got into the habit!

I had found that in this hospital it was the custom in Indian wards that, before doing a dressing, a towel should be put over the patient's face. This was the idea that what the eye doesn't see the mind doesn't grieve over. I found the truth of this when, one morning on my dressing list, I saw instructions to dress "Drainage tube in patient's abdomen". After taking off the old dressing, I could find no drainage tube to redress. There was a scar from the operation but that was all. I felt perplexed, and re-read my instructions, looked at his stomach again, and then went off to fetch Sister. She repeated the performance and went and fetched the M.O. He, too, was just as surprised. "Just as well the patient can't see," I thought, "or he would be getting worried." So then he was sent down to the theatre, and on opening him up again, the surgeon found that the tube had slipped inside. The whole thing was re-done and the tube stitched firmly in place. The patient, of course, never knew why he had had two operations. If he had, he might have become quite ill at the thought of it.

One of the patients had a worm in his leg, a kind that I had never come across before. He had an open sore in his ankle where it had got in and the M.O. explained to me that it would grow and grow right up his leg. The first morning, he showed me what to do. First, the man's leg was soaked for half an hour in salt water. Then the M.O. got hold of the end of the worm with pincers and pulled very gently until there was enough to wind around a match stick and then plaster it across. He was very careful, for if it broke, the worm would die and calcify in the man's leg.

Each day, I soaked the foot in more salt water and gently wound up another inch or two of fine, thin, worm. Finally, the worm got so fed up with the whole thing and being wound up on a match stick, that it slithered itself out into the bowl. It was astonishing and was so long it must have been right up in the man's thigh. I felt as proud as punch at having got it out successfully.

While gazing at it, I realised that an unknown officer was standing by me. It turned out to be an old friend of Bob's, Walter Ogilvie, who had called in to see me. He must have been surprised at the sight of Bob's future wife, down on her knees by her patient, and gazing with satisfaction at a long, thin worm.

Walter came to our Mess that evening for a drink and a talk. He had been a rubber planter near Moulmein before the war, and now was back with CAS. B. to help get Burmese affairs going again. He had visited his estate and his old cook had told him that he had taken Walter's family silver for safe keeping at the Buddhist temple. There the priest had hidden it, and later he was given it all safely back. He had also met Myra and Jean at

Moulmein and gave us news of them. Originally Walter had escaped from Burma via the Imphal route. He drove his car as far as possible and then walked the rest of that fearful treck across the Frontier Hills and into India. He didn't talk of this then, nor very rarely, later.

I had a letter from Bob in which he described a narrow escape he had had. There was one of these terrific tropical thunderstorms with forked lightning. One of these flashes had killed a sepoy standing only a few feet from him, and Bob himself, had been thrown up into the air.

He also said that he was learning to play Bridge for my sake, but hoped he wouldn't have to do too much of it. He enclosed a message from his Mess. "In spite of sacrificial efforts on the part of members of this Mess, he is making no progress in the scientific game called Bridge. So much so that stakes have been reduced to three Pice per 100. However, do not despair for we shall eventually make him a worthy partner for you – in this respect only."

On the 17th, I put in for marriage leave in November. At 10.15 a.m. on the 20th, Dorothy came to the ward to say that she had just heard that she was off next day by troopship, with two Sisters neither of whom wished to go as they preferred to fly in November. I dashed down to Major Robertson to ask if it was true, and might I go instead?

Straightaway he said he would telephone the Principal Matron, and in five minutes she had given her permission. He then took addresses to send wires and signals to Bob, and also Vera, to warn her that I was coming. Both he and the Assistant Matron were absolutely marvellous about it. He told me that officially I should return to 49. for my release, but added with a wink that he was sure that I could arrange something in Calcutta. I was quite honest that I was leaving and was touched at how nice everyone was to me about it. The Assistant Matron told me, "Get married and go to Ceylon with your husband. No one can stop you."

15

We had to have our luggage at the docks by 3 p.m. that day to be loaded on to the ship. Luckily, we had already packed our boxes but there was all the bedding and camp equipment to be done up and so many last minute things. Then all three on to a truck and down to the docks, where we left our baggage by 3 p.m. For Freda was sad at our going and had got permission for an immediate Leave and to join us two on the ship. When in a month she returned, she was the only remaining V.A.D. of our original ten, at 49. I.G.H.

We stayed the night at the Y.W. but were taken to a farewell party ending at the Officers' Club. We neither of us felt up to it, but something had to be done to celebrate our last evening in Rangoon.

Next day, down to the docks only to be told that the ship hadn't even arrived! There had been very bad weather with typhoons, and shipping had been delayed. So, back to the Y.W. for another three nights – such an anti-climax after having said goodbyes already. I sent off more wires, one to Vera about the delay, and another to Bob. Another letter had come from him complaining about not hearing from me, and now he was on the move again. So would any of these wires or signals ever reach him, I wondered.

One evening, we went to a farewell dinner with Colonel Jock Macdonald. He was such a nice old boy – a true Highland gentleman. He helped us to the last, sending his jeep to take us to the Swimming Club and which I drove for the last time. He also produced a tin trunk which Bob had left with him when he had gone by air for Central Burma.

Twenty five years later, I met Colonel Jock in Skye. He was wearing the kilt and full highland gear, and looked a very different figure from the shabby one in jungle green battledress.

He didn't remember me, but I hadn't forgotten his past kindness.

Eventually, the ship came in. We went aboard and were given a lovely luxurious cabin for two. The voyage was ghastly and we were prostrate for three whole days amidst squalls, rough seas, and we were a day late avoiding a cyclone. As we got into the shelter of the Hooglhi River, we all gradualy emerged, rather the worse for wear.

The Irwins gave me a warm welcome. Bobs Irwin was off to Delhi the next Sunday, so they had arranged for our wedding to be the day before on Saturday, and it was already Tuesday. The service was to be in a chapel of the Cathedral and then a small reception in the Bengal Club afterwards. The whole thing must have been a "Bride's Mother's" nightmare. Bride arrives five days late, with no wedding dress or anything warm for the honey-moon in Darjeeling. Worst of all, not a word from the bride-groom.

However, Vera took it all very calmly and efficiently. A brigadier friend sent a personal signal to Bob for them. However, not liking to sound like a shot-gun wedding, he didn't say that it was already arranged, so Bob had no idea of the urgency. Hoping to get a lift by air at least part of the way, he signalled back "arriving Friday". However, he had no priority and was not able to get a quick flight, and so started the long journey by road to Dimapur and then on by train.

Dorothy and Harry arranged to stay in Calcutta until Sunday so that he could be Best Man. Very nice of them, but I think they got quite a bit of entertainment out of it all. Bob had told me that he must be one of the worst dressed majors in the Army, as all he had was his jungle green battledress. So Harry, in his capacity of Best Man, forced open the tin trunk that they had taken charge of, and found a presentable jacket and trousers which they took to the cleaners to be ready for his wedding suit.

On Thursday morning, Vera took me in hand and we whizzed round getting me equipped. First the tailor where I chose some white material for a short dress. Then a suit and greatcoat to match, out of three green army blankets that I had bought in the Officers' Shop in Rangoon, made out of a fine pure wool from Australia. All these he promised to have ready by Saturday morning. Then the jewellers to order a ring; a hat shop for a flowered little hat; white shoes and, finally, the florist to order sprays and carnations.

Vera, in a letter to my mother, said that it had reminded her of their shopping together for her own wedding. I don't think that there could really have been much comparison with those leisured days. I just remember one mad rush and without Vera's help, I could never have done it.

On Friday, I went for fittings at the tailor, and then on to Howrah Station to meet Bob. All that was needed now was the bridegroom, but when the train came in, he wasn't on it. I waited for the second train and he wasn't on that either. I then went round to Dorothy's, where Harry got out the gin bottle and gave me a very strong one.

Vera appeared to take it all very calmly – or anyway for my sake did. She must have had some doubts herself, though I, myself, never thought Bob wouldn't eventually turn up. She gave me a strong drink too; in fact I must have consumed a lot of gin that week. Later the Brigadier telephoned that he had had a second signal to say that Bob was arriving on Sunday.

So, Vera got busy again postponing everything until Monday, Bobs Irwin wouldn't be there, but it was a public holiday and the rest of the guests would be able to come. Harry rounded up a fellow officer staying in the Grand to take over his duties as Best Man. The Bengal club was already fully booked, but she changed everything for a small reception in her garden. She even got me a hair appointment for Monday morning. At least Saturday was now free for me to collect my clothes and get my breath back. All was ready and we just waited for the groom.

On Sunday morning, I arrived early at Howrah Station and walked once or twice up the platform, passing a platoon of Indian sepoys. Suddenly there was a shout of "Sister Sahib" and running footsteps. I turned to see that one of the sepoys had broken ranks and was running down the platform after me. He stopped and saluted, "Sister Sahib, Panitola Hospital. Das No. Ward." This was an old patient, from a year ago, and he had even recognised me out of uniform. Fortunately I was able to explain to the horrified havildar who had raced after him. For my Urdu had improved, and I could ask after the man's health better than the old "thik hai" of my first days at Panitola. I noticed people around were staring and wondering what was up, but the Old Patient situation was one I had got used to. It was a happy little incident that stood out in the haze of the last few days.

The train came in, and Bob stepped off, and from then on everything went as it should. We lunched with Dorothy and Harry and met the new Best Man. Then on to the Cathedral to see the Padre, who advised us to have a large family – a cricket eleven– if possible which left us both a little speechless.

We then returned in triumph to Vera and I expect we all had some more strong drinks. Her husband had left for Delhi, but the two P.G.s had great fun choosing unsuitable hymns for us like "Six days have we laboured" and hymns for those "in stress and strain."

Next day the wedding was at 4 p.m. The Bridegroom was in good time. The Bride a customary ten minutes late. The service was simple, the high spot being the hymns where the congregation of eight made more noise than any choir, and the Padre got so enthused he went into a descant. I had unaccustomed high heels, and my knees shook and I was afraid I would topple over.

Vera must have been pleased with the result of all her hard work and organising and reorganising. I know how grateful I was to her for her thoughtfulness. We dined at Firpos and caught the Night Mail for Darjeeling.

We stayed at the Mount Everest. A huge hotel but, being out of season, rather cold and bleak. I wrote home that it felt bitterly cold after Rangoon, "but we have been so happy, that we haven't really cared."

From Darjeeling, we could see the snow capped Himalayas, with the towering height of Mount Kangchinjunga, which, at times, appeared to float over the clouds below. It was very beautiful. Here we were among the Nepalese, the people from whom our Gurkha troops were recruited. I saw how strong the women were and how they carried great weights on their heads as though they were nothing.

There were locally made fur coats, and Bob chose me a Himalayan Fox. It was gorgeously warm and how lovely to need warm clothes again.

We hired ponies and trotted round the Darjeeling roads. There were lovely walks and always that breathtaking view of the mountains.

The Agah Khan and his new French wife arrived to stay in our hotel. There was a reception for them with the Indian band playing and crowds out to watch. It was a steep path up to the hotel entrance so the Aga Khan, looking very dignified, was brought up in a carrying chair. His nearly six foot tall wife walked beside him, very statuesque and beautiful. On arrival, they were garlanded and the band played a cheerful tune. It was as well that we were probably the only people to know the words. "See that collar and tie – don't he look a guy." After their arrival, the bath water became hot instead of tepid, and we hoped they would stay for the whole of our visit.

Bob, in his excitement at leaving to get married, had left his Mepacrine tablets at Imphal and also forgot to tell me. Soon he sprang a temperature and there he was with Malaria. A doctor staying in the hotel gave him tablets, and told me "routine fever treatment". So, there I was giving my husband tepid sponges to get his temperature down. However, by now I wasn't surprised at anything.

I heard from Vera, very apologetic about my letters. Such a huge pile had arrived for me that she had done them up to be sent by registered post. The chaprassi took them to the Post Office and a thief, seeing him queueing up with what must be a valuable packet to be registered, snatched it and ran off. She had indentified some of the letters as being from my family, but was amazed at the number of men writing to me from England. Their names were on the back of the envelopes and were of all ranks and regiments. I realised that they must be our special smallpox ward patients writing from boardship. They had said, "We shall all be writing to you, Nurse". They probably had, and now I didn't know their addresses. Nor did I know who had written to me and who had not, among those friends that I lost contact with. It was very sad, but most of all I regretted never answering any of the P.O.W.s letters.

16

While in Darjeeling, we heard little news. No wireless and few papers. We hadn't heard that civil disturbances had started with "Quit India" riots. We arrived back at Calcutta early in the morning and found there were no taxis and were told that they were all on strike. So we hired a horse-drawn gharri to take us to the Grand Hotel.

The streets were strangely empty, but the sidewalks crowded with Indians who just stood and stared at us in complete silence. The silence was disconcerting. Indian wards were noisy, but friendly places. Now, all these Indians just stared with hatred in their faces, and all seemed to be waiting for something to happen. We neither of us spoke a word in case we should break this waiting silence. It was a long drive from the station and, that morning, seemed very long indeed. To me, it all seemed unbelievable. I had never seen hatred on an Indian's face before. I remembered the sepoy who broke ranks at the Station to come and greet me; our wardfulls of Indian patients; the Indian staff, from the doctors down, who treated us with respect and liking. Now, here was this terrible hatred from people who had never seen us before.

A year later, these same crowds turned on their fellow-Indians, because they were Mohammedans, and there was terrible slaughter in Calcutta. Many Englishmen drove their own cars and fetched their Mohammedan staff and families to live in safety in the European offices. In what is now Pakistan and Bangladesh, they turned on the Hindus and there was the same slaughter – all in the name of religion.

We finally reached the Grand and paid our driver well for his courage in bringing us. We found all public transport had been stopped and no one was allowed out of the hotel. From our room, we watched Chowringhee – the big wide street outside.

There were hundreds and thousands of Indians milling around. One solitary taxi, flying an American flag, tried to drive through, but the mob stopped it and pulled the soldiers out. They shouted furiously that they were Americans, but that didn't mean anything to the excited crowds around. Then some American police went in brandishing their pistols like in a gangster film, and cleared a way for the G.I.s to get through.

By next day things had quietened down and Bob took me out to the Irwins, before leaving again for Imphal. It was peaceful out in Alipore, with little sight or sounds of the riots in Calcutta city. These 'Quit India' riots were mainly against the Military. Public transport had been stopped, but Bobs Irwin and the other two men drove to work as usual in their own civilian cars.

That evening Vera and I took her little dog for a walk along the quiet road that ran along the back of their garden. Suddenly a gang of men came round the corner and started shouting at us.

"I think we had better turn around now," said Vera as she stooped and fastened the lead to her dog. "Don't hurry. Just walk with me."

Why don't they call the military out?" I asked, feeling rather frightened.

"They never do if they can possibly help it. It is something that one learns to live with. These men are probably not the real rioters, but hooligans hoping for loot. Remember," she said, "the great thing is never to show fear."

I was thankful when we reached the safety of our garden, but on glancing back, I saw that though still shouting abuse, the men had not followed us.

Vera told me that many civilians worried that we Service girls, newly out from England, might, out of sheer ignorance, behave foolishly and so trigger off really bad riots.

Now the war was over, Bob Irwin had been granted Leave to England in the very near future. Their successors were taking over the house in a week's time, so it was vital for me to report to the Medical Authorities. Next day Bobs gave me a lift into Calcutta and dropped me off in the Fort. I promised that I would ask the Army for a lift back.

I saw the D.A.D.M.S. to explain my position, and he couldn't have been nicer saying that of course I would get my release. In the meantime he said, I could be attached to a Military Hospital in Calcutta and work there. He telephoned the Principal Matron for confirmation but, to my horror, she said, "No," and that I must return to Rangoon and apply through my own hospital. V.A.D.s were now the only women's service in India who didn't get automatic release on marriage – only as a concession if their husbands returned to England. He was sympathetic, and advised me to make an appointment to see her myself.

While I was in the Fort, rioting had become more serious and at last the military was called out. Everywhere troops were arming, then jumping into trucks and off to patrol the streets. A visiting officer took compassion on me and said that he would give me a lift to the Grand, but refused to take me any further. So I was stuck in the hotel all day, though able to telephone Vera to say what had happened.

Once the troops were out, Calcutta quietened down again. After tea I managed to get a lift in an Army truck that was taking the hotel's Anglo-Indian employees home. Afterwards it took me on to Alipore, where the Irwins were certainly relieved to see me. The three men had all arrived back safely, but now they were wondering what to do about me. But no one was surprised that the armed troops in the back of my truck belonged to an Indian regiment, as I couldn't have been under safe guard.

The Mail had come and I found a letter from 49 I.G.H. posting me as ABSENT WITHOUT LEAVE. Help! The new Matron must have arrived full of Base Hospital discipline and Red Tape. My situation was getting difficult. The Irwins would be leaving for England and when, oh when, was Bob going to get his release? When he did, he would certainly be annoyed if I had gone back to Rangoon.

Probably out of sheer worry and nerves, I sprang a temperature, and there was the solution. I was admitted to the British General Hospital as a patient and I couldn't have gone to a better place. The Sisters were sweet and the Matron, herself, wrote to the Principal Matron, 12th Army, at Rangoon. She pointed out that, as my hospital was already packing up for the next move on, it would save them trouble if I was given my release in Calcutta.

In the meantime she ordered me Sick-leave at the Lady Mary Herbert Hostel.

That is what happened, and eventually a letter came through from the D.M.S., 12th Army, for me to apply for release in triplicate. What a relief. My unorthodox way of leaving must have given poor Miss Corsar one more headache, but she forgave me. For several months later, long after leaving India, I heard from the Red Cross with my discharge, and enclosed were my campaign medals and the thanks of King and Country.

I had only to wait a week or two before Bob arrived back in Calcutta, and we left on a four day train journey to Ceylon, and a new and very different life. I took with me grateful memories of the Matrons and Q.A. sisters who had been so kind and helpful to me at the end.

17

It was in Ceylon, or Sri Lanka as it is now called, that our two daughters were born. They are the eighth generation of my family to have been born, or worked, out East. But then we broke the pattern. We returned to England in 1958, and our girls grew up and married here. It is in this country that our grandchildren have been born.

The world is changing so. When their descendents grow up, where will they spread their wings? Will there be Space Ships for them to fly in? Will they travel and settle in New Worlds? Only time can give the answer.

It is for these children that I have written this story about the 14th Army. It had been a truly International army, made up of many races – our own British troops, and those from India, Pakistan, Bangladesh, Africa, the Gurkhas from Nepal, and last but certainly not least, the courageous support from the Air-forces of both Britain and the U.S.A. Each man so proud of his own regiment, but all fighting in harmony under one flag – the Union Jack.

I write the story too, of some of the British girls who went out to India to help nurse in the hospitals of the 'Forgotten Army.' How they, and the Queen Alexandria Sisters, did their best for all races, regardless of caste or religion. It is almost History now. One day these children may read this with interest, and say, "They were my Grandparents," and be proud of it.

REPORT ON V.A.D. UNIT IN INDIA JANUARY 1945
by G. Corsar
Chief Liaison Officer

Locality

All members are at present working in what is known as the Forward Areas. The 250 are divided between eleven hospitals, many were working with the 14th Army. The 14th has now moved on but these hospitals have so far remained stationary and now come under the L. of C. (Lines of communication) command, catering for regiments moving up into Burma, sick and wounded passing back. Four of these hospitals are just on the border of the Arakan, in the Chittagong hill tract, east of the Bay of Bengal. There are others northwards thoughout Assam following up along the India Burma border, through Imphal to the Manipur road and Kohima. (A beautiful spot right up in the hills) A very isolated bit of country which was over-run by the Japs last Spring – Johat, Dibrugarh, Panitola and, furthest north of all, Ledo, where we have recently posted 7 members. Very primitive conditions, and grand work being done by these Members who had to tackle a very tough job. Much Typhus coming in – the type producing very high fever and subsequent weakness. Much careful nursing required but all such as V.A.D.s can do.

Then further south west at Gauhati, a large hospital of 1,000 or more beds, where there is much work and much responsibility for our people. Also in Sylhet, south central Assam. Others not quite so far forward, but equally large and busy hospitals, are two near Comilla and two at Agartala about 60 miles north of Comilla. All these hospitals are in the S.E. Asia command. We have only three back in India: 2 in Ranchi, and one in Dacca.

Quarters

Approximately 75% are living in Bashas, ie huts built of bamboo interlaced with matting. Thatched roofs, floors of brick, cement, or just mud. Some are fitted with electric light and fans, others not so fortunate use hurricane lamps. One unit is in tents, others in more substantial buildings.

Amenities

Shops are practically nil. Officer's shops are the only ones for replenishing garments etc. There is usually one in the district but, in some cases, from 10 to 15 miles distant. No other shops within reach except small Indian bazaars.

There is evidence in every place of the necessity of fully equipping members before posting to Forward areas.

In nearly every case there is a Club of sorts in the area – tennis, dancing, cinema. Invitations from neighbouring Messes are innumerable.

Patients

Chiefly Indian 'other ranks', often some West Africans, some British as well as Officers, both British and Indian. The majority of our people really love nursing the Indian – he is very child-like and quite pathetic when sick and shows much gratitude for all that is done for him.

Duties

These girls are doing a magnificent job. They have very great responsibilities – really rather alarming to begin with and many matrons have told me that on first arrival they had not got much sense of responsibility but that they were growing up to it remarkably well. Certainly when I went around the units in December I was absolutely amazed to learn what they were doing and to see how remarkably well they tackle their jobs. I usually found members working opposite each other with one large ward each with several side wards attached with dangerously ill persons or Africans as opposed to Indians etc. One sister would be in charge of this block and if she is off duty they have to appeal to the next block if a sister is required. They carry on with ordinary, routine ward duties, doing all dressings and nursing treatments as instructed by the sisters. Many are working on penicillin wards which new treatment is doing such marvellous work now in clearing up septic cases. It involves giving intramuscular injections three-hourly throughout the day and night. Other members are working in casualty theatres. Those who have had much previous experience in any particular branch are getting the opportunity of making use of that experience. We have some who have worked for two or three years in the theatres in England, these members are now finding themselves in the theatre out here. Sometimes, with simple cases, if the sister is off duty, they are even working on their own for surgeons. I saw another giving anaesthetics. Those experienced in TB are in TB wards; opthalmic people posted where there is opthalmic work etc.

Night-Duty

The most severe responsibilities rest on members during this period of night-duty. Because of the strain of this they never do more than a fortnight at a time. One girl told me she had three hundred patients in three different blocks including, of course, many seriously ill. The sister on call visited her twice nightly, otherwise she was alone with just the help of nursing sepoys who themselves require a good deal of supervision. There are many who, as soon as the nurse's back is turned, curl up and go to sleep under a table or in a corner! Besides doing her rounds and all treatments, this member had three different reports to write during the night. Another tells me of her 138 patients with only a sister on call in case of emergency. Another had six blocks to look after with a sister on call. This is not merely going around from ward to ward all under one roof. She had an old Indian coolie who carried her hurricane lamp, and together they ploughed their way through the sand or in the rain through the mud, sometimes up and down hills, amongst trees, from one block of buildings to another.

Mess Duty

V.A.D. members are working in their respective messes thus entirely relieving a fully trained sister for ward work. They are extraordinarily good about this working in the home and on enquiries from me, although they admit they are disappointed not to be working in the ward, yet they do see if they can set a fully trained sister free that it is a worth while job. I have not had one single grouse about this. Two of these are married women who have run their own homes in India before the war and speak the language fluently and understand the servants. They are, of course, proving invaluable to the matrons, and all by their cheerful and friendly manner in the home, doing valuable work for us drawing sisters and V.A.D.s together. The sisters are, on the whole, on most friendly terms with our members.

Social Problems

Members are gradually finding their level. Learning how many engagements they are capable of keeping in a week. They started by going out far too frequently, not always for the love of gaiety but because they had not learned the art of refusing invitations without feeling embarrassed about causing offence. Some were thus getting over-tired. Some localities, more in Assam, are presenting great problems for young members. They have extreme difficulty in keeping apart from the type of men with whom, for very good reason, they do not wish to associate. Young married members always present a problem. With all the good-will they can muster, it is found that being in the same country as their husbands, and yet unable to live together, does from the psychological side have a very disturbing effect which is only aggravated by a short leave spent together. There must of necessity be the anxiety as to whether both parties will get their next leave to coincide. Is their leave to be cancelled if a rush of work comes? Can she be loyal to her unit and not press to be allowed to go and yet know that her husband will have to spend his leave alone and not be available when she is free? All this presents so much anxiety to the young marrieds that no matter how hard they might fight against it, it seems in some cases to cause real nervous strain. Some have themselves discussed these problems freely with me.

General Morale

Home-sickness is conspicuous by its absence. Enthusiasm is very real and very great. Enjoyment of the life in India is also very real and very great. General morale is most excellent. I find these members, apart from enjoying their work (and pay), are so particularly delighted to find that there seems to be a real place for V.A.D.s in India – a gap which they can really fill. Perhaps their greatest pleasure and relief is to find that they are made welcome by the sisters, both in the hospitals and in the mess. In my opinion after having visited all units and spoken to every member individually, I find they are as a whole putting all they have into the work they came out to do. They are tremendously enthusiastic. The more work they have, the better they are pleased. The further forward they are towards the battle zone the better they are pleased. Should the conditions not be so good, they accept what there is with pleasure, and consider themselves lucky to be chosen to go to those more active fields of service. I was asked time and again if they could be sent further forward. There is a general longing to be attached to the 14th Army and move out with it wherever and whenever it moves. Shops, good quarters, clubs and dances, or proximity to trains and buses all take a very small place in comparison to the possibilities that lie ahead of hospital service. This is not meant to hide the fact that the majority of members are, when off duty, having a thoroughly good time and making the most of it; but it is meant to show that the opinion I have formed is that with very few exceptions they are putting the hospital work definitely first. I formed this opinion from what matrons say, as well as what V.A.D.s tell me. They speak universally of a kindness received and are full of appreciation of the welcome accorded them in hospitals.

Liaison Officers

My headquarters are at G.H.Q. in New Delhi – Miss Hoare, the senior of my two assistants was first sent to G.H.Q. Medical Branch, A.L.L.S.E.A., (Allied Land Forces South East Asia) under their chief principal matron near Calcutta. Miss Neald, my junior assistant, works under the principal matron of L. of C. (Lines of Communication). Comilla – northerly point of Bay of Bengal, very hot and humid district. All initial postings are done by me at the request and subject to the approval of the chief principal matron (Miss Patterson) with whom I work closely. I keep all V.A.D.s' personal files, record cards, etc., in my office, and all V.A.D. correspondence. I do of course get crowds of letters from members asking advice on all and sundry subjects (I wish some would ask for more!) I receive and answer all correspondence under D.O.L. (Demi Official Letter) rate as these do not have to pass through official channels and nobody knows how many I receive or write! Members have not yet learned to make sufficient use of the matrons who would give more help if asked, and owing to distance, post time would be saved as some of these letters take ten days to reach me. I have an understanding with Miss Neald by which she sends me a weekly report of happenings in her area – this weekly letter tells me much more and keeps me in close touch.

All staff at G.H.Q. are most charming to me and are becoming very cooperative. I have every confidence that no matter how many more members are sent out to India they will be welcomed and find equally good work awaiting them. G.J.S. *Corsar*, V.A.D. *Liaison Officer (India) January, 1945.*

SECOND REPORT ON V.A.D. UNIT IN INDIA. SEPTEMBER 1946

I gave my last report of the Indian Unit in January 1945, and returned to India a few weeks later. I was sent back to England for two or three weeks in order to assist in recruiting a further 500. By April of that year, the results of the frantic efforts of the previous months to get more members released for India began to bear fruit.

April, June, August, September and October, each brought draughts out to us varying from 45 to 145 nursing members: by October the majority of hospitals were well staffed but the urgent call for more sisters was also carrying in effect.

In the meantime war had stopped and the expected invasion of Singapore never took place – thus the stream of wounded for which we were preparing fortunately never materialised and so there was a lull and the next move was not to draught people into S.E.A.C. (South East Asia Command) but to muster them in the base hospitals of India to which the P.O.W.s were to be brought, chiefly Bangalore and Secunderabad.

In November it was a joy to go to Bombay and meet the first draft of real military V.A.D.s (200 more were released from military hospitals in the U.K. and B.L.A. for India and thus many were with this draft of 145). They were intensely keen and their training as regards discipline and adaptability certainly showed itself. Almost all wanted to get far afield and to go forward into S.E.A.C. and it was quite distressing to see their disappointment at hearing the need was no longer in that area. In fact their disappointment was only to be accentuated when they arrived at their units to find the patients were few and hospitals were fully staffed.

I know of at least one instance at a C.C.S. (Casualty Clearing Station) at which on their arrival four keen young members were met by the sister in charge with "What have you come for? I don't want you. Got too many in the mess already!" I can think of no more depressing welcome at the end of four days' train journey across India and it is greatly to their credit that those members settled into that mess with such patience and tact that, by the time I visited them three months later, that sister in charge could not speak too highly of them, they were obviously the most popular members of that mess. My members arrived in November and even in February 1946 a final 11 arrived, thus making our total 769 including the three officers. By this time we had members serving throughout the whole of India and S.E.A.C. They served altogether in 118 different units including four C.C.S. and four hospital ships. They were to be found in hospitals from Bombay district in the West as afar as Sumatra, Java and Hong Kong in the East. From way up in the North-West Frontier, Peshawar and districts down to Ceylon.

Due to having to go to Bombay so frequently in order to meet the newcomers, I was not able personally to visit all hospitals but I travelled as extensively as time would permit between these Bombay visits and thanks to the opportunity afforded me of getting to know all these members on their arrival I was able to keep up a lively correspondence with them all. I received and answered over 1,000 letters from individual members during those two years.

During 1944 and the early part of 1945 matrons had not known where to turn for staff. Then came the sudden influx of both sisters and V.A.D.s together with the cessation of hostilities. Thus each mess was accommodating more staff than it could comfortably hold and it was difficult to find sufficient work in many of the hospitals. These slack months were difficult ones for the unit as a whole. The war was over. Many people's thoughts turned to home and future careers etc. Slack units always breed discontent and such letters came in almost daily. "The war is over – I signed on for the duration. Why cannot I go home?" Forgetting that the contract was for "The duration of the present emergency," not war. Or "My husband is demobilised back in his peacetime job in India and wants me at home to run the bungalow." All married women are getting their release. What about us?" Or "I left a busy hospital in B.L.A. and came out here to find I am not wanted. Can't I go back where I did feel of some use?"

All suchlike requests and the many petty complaints would never have been thought of if people had been busy. All these required definite and reasonable answers which would satisfy the enquirers as to the rights and wrongs of the particular case. With amazingly few exceptions, they took and accepted those replies with, in my opinion, extraordinary grace and courage. Then came the turn of the tide. The present emergency was said to be over in April. There was some discussion as to how and when this unit would be disbanded. By January and February we were all desperately anxious to be given some definite idea regarding our future. It was distressing to have to reply: "We do not yet know" to so many enquiries. India Office and G.H.Q. did not seem to be able to come to any definite decision. In February we were greatly helped by the arrival in Delhi of Lady Louis Mountbatten, who stood for no more hesitation on this matter. A decision had to be reached, and reached to-day and published this week.

It was difficult to know whether to dispense with only the original members or to close down the whole unit: sending them all back as soon as passages could be procured on the "first come first to go home" system. There was some thought of letting each member complete eighteen months or one year in India irrespective of whether they were still essentially required in hospitals. It was, however, thought not to be to the good of the morale or prestige of the unit if members found themselves as extras in a sisters' mess.

The question was therefore put to the Adjutant General in India direct by Lady Louis, "Will your hospitals be adequately staffed if all V.A.D.s go? Do you still need them to supplement your staff?" His reply was, "No the time has now come when we can dispense with them. More hospitals are closing every month. Hundreds of sisters arrived out during the last few months and the records of sickness in the army show a lower percentage that we have ever known. As far as the working of hospitals is concerned, we do not now need them."

This was the deciding factor. I was fully in agreement with Lady Louis that under these circumstances the unit should be disbanded. It had served its purpose and now this work should go to the Indian Military Nursing Service and the Auxiliary Nursing Service India whose members we had been supplementing.

As the officer in charge of this unit, I also had been taking a keen interest in the state of things in general in India and felt very keenly that it was no longer going to be a healthy place for any surplus women. If there is an essential job for them to do out here, well and good, and if not they should go as soon as no longer required.

All commands were notified that V.A.D.s were now due for immediate release and that passages would be procured as soon as available.

I was given to understand that there might be three or four months delay after abdication had been made: it was therefore a very great astonishment that full allocations were given according to requests for April, May and June.

Now my daily post-bag took a turn in the opposite direction.

Instead of "Can't I go, must I stay?" it was "Can't I stay, must I go?" Letters, telegrams and cables poured in.

Many tried to get civilian work in India but (I think fortunately) this proved unavailable. Untold numbers wanted release in India. But all applications for this had to go up to the joint repatriation office for approval and he passed none unless they either had husbands or their parents in the country, or could give definite date of marriage within the next few weeks, or proof of definite and satisfactory employment.

There was much disappointment especially among the more recent arrivals. I do however think that, the more they discussed it with civilians, the more did they begin to realise that India is not a good spot for unattached women these days.,

In April I went to Bombay and saw the first draft on board their ship bound for home (Approximately 200).

They went on the first to come first to go system. The majority of this draft were, I think, quite pleased with the thought of home. Many were ready for a rest and I had few, if any, complaints.

In May I went again to Bombay and saw another large draft off. This draft included many who had been out but a few months and there was a good deal of disappointment over their return although these members also as a whole saw the disadvantage of taking their release in India.

It was of very great interest to me having met and got to know these members on their arrival to be able to meet and chat with them again at the end of their time – not only to hear of their many most interesting experiences but to notice the effect of those months upon their various personalities: some for better some for worse: but I felt confident in saying that in the majority of cases it was for the better. Their growth in self-reliance, personality and general strength of character showed itself in a most amazing way. I could see that in their faces, let alone their speech and bearing, and one felt that many were returning better fitted for the task that lies ahead going out into the world for the first time as individuals to look for and start their chosen careers. So many were there who had come more or less straight from school into the service and they were returning as fully developed young women whose presence would make itself felt.

The final draft left with Miss Neald in June. I was sorry to see our part come to an end. She had been an invaluable assistant to me and I shall always be grateful for her loyalty and sense of humour.

This finished our unit as far as India was concerned. Those in South East Asia Command sailed independently from ports in S.E.A.C., Singapore, Rangoon and Colombo.

Their departure passed through the hands of Miss Hoare who has throughout taken the bulk of the responsibility of S.E.A.C. – though she was good enough to keep me informed of all movements. I have been entirely dependent upon her for personal news of those members and she has put in an enormous amount of excellent and conscientious work visiting or writing to those in that area. I have much to thank her for, in that she has kept me so completely, in touch with everything throughout. She served in Rangoon, Ceylon and Singapore.

The members from her area also went home as far as possible in the same order they came out, she herself being the last to leave.

I stayed on at G.H.Q. until I had all records completed and could account for every member of the entire unit of 769.

I left Delhi on the 18th July, at that time there were still eleven

V.A.D.s on the books not yet having been struck off strength from their units. These were all awaiting ships to take them to various countries to which they had already obtained permission for release.

I cannot close this report without making mention of the unfailing kindness and cooperation I have always received from the D.M.S. (Director Medical Service) General Wilson, and his successor General Thompson and the chief principal matron Miss Patterson. She never once let any single thing concerning V.A.D.s pass through her office without calling me and discussing it freely with me and I always felt that I was working under a wonderfully sympathetic chief with a real understanding of V.A.D.s and one to whom I could always turn for help and advice.

I should also like to mention the friendly cooperation I received from the principal matron Indian Military Nursing Service. This was rather contrary to my expectations it was therefore real joy when I found I had her full support. Many are the times I turned to her for advice and never once failed to receive it coupled with wholehearted friendship.

Needless to say our mainstay throughout was our continued backing from London. To know that constant help and support which was always ours from the V.A.D. standing committee meant just everything.

To feel that they had kept a finger on the map of India throughout and took such a vital and personal interest in each one of us certainly made my life as liaison officer a real joy, and removed any feeling of being overburdened with unsurmountable difficulties. For I could not have had better support and encouragement than that brought to be by air mails frequently from London. G.J.S. *Corsar* V.A.D. *Liaison Officer India 19th September, 1946.*

P.S. At the end of our time in India I was sitting in the garden of the hotel in which I was staying in Delhi, when a senior officer of the British Military Police came and sat beside me. He said "I would like you to know that your V.A.D.s caused us less trouble than any of the other women's services in India." I thanked him and said that this was a great tribute to the British Red Cross.

I therefore feel I should add this foot note to my report on our India unit.